Getting Started with SQL Server 2014 Administration

Optimize your database server to be fast, efficient, and highly secure using the brand new features of SQL Server 2014

Gethyn Ellis

BIRMINGHAM - MUMBAI

Getting Started with SQL Server 2014 Administration

First published: April 2014

Production Reference: 1180414

Published by Packt Publishing Ltd.
Livery Place
35 Livery Street
Birmingham B3 2PB, UK.

ISBN 978-1-78217-241-3

www.packtpub.com

Cover Image by Karl Moore (karl@karlmoore.co.uk)

Credits

Author
Gethyn Ellis

Reviewers
Brenner Grudka Lira
David Loo
Richard Louie

Commissioning Editor
Antony Lowe

Acquisition Editors
Richard Harvey
Antony Lowe

Content Development Editor
Arun Nadar

Technical Editors
Aman Preet Singh
Nachiket Vartak

Copy Editors
Mradula Hegde
Gladson Monteiro
Adithi Shetty

Project Coordinator
Lima Danti

Proofreader
Maria Gould

Indexers
Mehreen Deshmukh
Mariammal Chettiyar

Graphics
Ronak Dhruv

Production Coordinator
Aparna Bhagat

Cover Work
Aparna Bhagat

About the Author

Gethyn Ellis is a SQL Server consultant and trainer with clients in Europe and North America. His client base includes both public and private sector clients that range from large financial firms to departments of the UK government. Specialized in database administration, virtualization, and performance, he has been involved in several large projects that involve migration of large SQL Server estates to the latest version of SQL Server and also migrated that infrastructure to a virtualized platform. He is also an instructor with Learning Tree and teaches several courses on the Learning Tree SQL Server curriculum. You can follow Gethyn's blog at www.gethynellis.com.

I would like to mention a few people here. My Mum, Lynda, and dad, Ron Ellis for encouraging me to write this book. My sister, Katheryn, and brother-in-law, Gareth Lewis, who have just given birth to twin boys. I would also like to mention my niece and two new nephews, Carys Gwen, Iwan, and Efan Lewis. Last but not least, I also wish to mention my two golden retriever dogs, Seth and Jake. While I wrote this book, these two helped me dearly by providing necessary distractions from the writing process by demanding regular long walks.

About the Reviewers

Brenner Grudka Lira has been a data analyst and DBA at NeuroTech since 2012. He has a bachelor's degree in Computer Science and a post graduate degree in Project Management, both from the Catholic University of Pernambuco, Recife, Brazil.

He also has experience in building and modeling data warehouses and has knowledge of SQL Server and MySQL database management. At present, he is dedicated to the study of project management and database tuning.

He has already reviewed the books *Microsoft SQL Server Denali Integration Services: An Expert Handbook* and *Oracle BI Publisher 11g: A Practical Guide to Enterprise Reporting*, both published by *Packt Publishing*.

David Loo is a senior software development professional with over 25 years of experience in both software development and people management. He is respected for his ability to focus teams on service excellence and for designing and implementing practical process improvements and solutions. He is always on the lookout for ways to contribute his knowledge and experience of software development, team building, and developing best practices.

Richard Louie is a Business Intelligence developer at Redwood Trust, a residential and commercial mortgage investment firm. He has extensive experience in Oracle and Microsoft SQL for ETL, SSIS, SSRS, SSAS, and VB.Net. He is an ASQ Green Belt certified professional and is a graduate of the University of California, Irvine, in Information and Computer Science. He has reviewed the book *Getting Started with SQL Server 2012 Cube Development*, *Packt Publishing*.

www.PacktPub.com

Support files, eBooks, discount offers and more

You might want to visit www.PacktPub.com for support files and downloads related to your book.

Did you know that Packt offers eBook versions of every book published, with PDF and ePub files available? You can upgrade to the eBook version at www.PacktPub.com and as a print book customer, you are entitled to a discount on the eBook copy. Get in touch with us at service@packtpub.com for more details.

At www.PacktPub.com, you can also read a collection of free technical articles, sign up for a range of free newsletters and receive exclusive discounts and offers on Packt books and eBooks.

http://PacktLib.PacktPub.com

Do you need instant solutions to your IT questions? PacktLib is Packt's online digital book library. Here, you can access, read and search across Packt's entire library of books.

Why Subscribe?

- Fully searchable across every book published by Packt
- Copy and paste, print and bookmark content
- On demand and accessible via web browser

Free Access for Packt account holders

If you have an account with Packt at www.PacktPub.com, you can use this to access PacktLib today and view nine entirely free books. Simply use your login credentials for immediate access.

Instant Updates on New Packt Books

Get notified! Find out when new books are published by following @PacktEnterprise on Twitter, or the *Packt Enterprise* Facebook page.

Table of Contents

Preface

SQL Server releases seem to be coming thick and fast these days. Since SQL Server 2005, there has been a new release nearly every two years. Most of the new features have had a business intelligence focus since SQL Server 2005. There have been some features that the production DBA that looks after transaction systems would have an interest in, such as the AlwaysOn Availability Groups feature introduced with SQL Server 2012. This new release of SQL Server has some great new features that will capture the attention of the database administrator "in the trenches". You will learn how to improve the performance of your transactional databases by utilizing the new In-Memory OLTP features. Cloud has been a buzz word for a quite a long time, and SQL Server 2014 allows closer integration with the cloud using Microsoft Azure. You can create complete virtual machines with SQL Server installed in Microsoft Azure or you can simply store your database files in the Microsoft Azure cloud.

What this book covers

Chapter 1, SQL Server 2014 and Cloud, will teach you how to make use of Microsoft Azure Storage to store the data files of your local instance databases in the cloud.

Chapter 2, Backup and Restore Improvements, will cover how to back up your database to a URL and Microsoft Azure Storage. It will also teach you to use native tools to encrypt your SQL Server backups.

Chapter 3, In-Memory Optimized Tables, explores the main new features of In-Memory OLTP, which can significantly improve performance of your transactional systems.

Chapter 4, Delayed Durability, offers the DBA the option of controlling how transactions are written to the transaction log. This setting can also significantly help improve the performance of your database.

Chapter 5, *AlwaysOn Availability Groups*, discusses the enhancements in AlwaysOn Availability groups and shows how you to set up a replica on Microsoft Azure Virtual Machine.

Chapter 6, *Performance Improvements*, covers some of the other new features and enhancements that can help improve performance.

What you need for this book

For this book, you will need the SQL Server 2014 software. If you want to set up and make use of the Microsoft Azure features, you will need a Microsoft Azure subscription. You can sign up for a free trial at http://azure.microsoft.com/en-us/. If you want to set up and explore the AlwaysOn Availability feature, you will need at least three virtual machines. I like to use VMware Fusion on my Mac, but you can use whichever hypervisor suits you.

Who this book is for

This book is for people who want to learn the new features of SQL Server 2014, especially database administrators and system administrators. In order to get the most out of this book, you need to have some previous experience in managing and administering a SQL Server instance.

Conventions

In this book, you will find a number of styles of text that distinguish between different kinds of information. Here are some examples of these styles, and an explanation of their meaning.

Code words in text, database table names, folder names, filenames, file extensions, pathnames, dummy URLs, user input, and Twitter handles are shown as follows: "Give the virtual machine a name. In my case, I have named my virtual machine GRESQL2014."

A block of code is set as follows:

```
CREATE DATABASE TestDB1
ON
(NAME = TestDB1_data,
    FILENAME = 'https://gresqlstorage.blob.core.windows.net/sqldata/
TestDB1Data.mdf')
  LOG ON
```

```
(NAME = TestDB1_log,
    FILENAME = 'https://gresqlstorage.blob.core.windows.net/sqldata/
TestDB1Log.ldf')
GO
```

Any command-line input or output is written as follows:

```
CREATE CREDENTIAL [https://gresqlstorage.blob.core.windows.net/sqldata]
WITH IDENTITY='SHARED ACCESS SIGNATURE',
SECRET = 'sr=c&si=SQLDATA&sig=PtQi1NXUuJz%2BGCUkpdgEBS4o4Lo60FjTbfJ2dNx3X
X8%3D'
```

New terms and **important words** are shown in bold. Words that you see on the screen, in menus or dialog boxes for example, appear in the text like this: "Click on the **SQL DATABASES** option in the left-hand side menu".

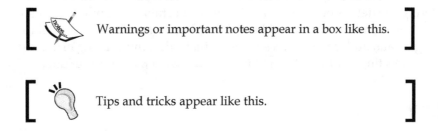

Warnings or important notes appear in a box like this.

Tips and tricks appear like this.

Reader feedback

Feedback from our readers is always welcome. Let us know what you think about this book—what you liked or may have disliked. Reader feedback is important for us to develop titles that you really get the most out of.

To send us general feedback, simply send an e-mail to feedback@packtpub.com, and mention the book title via the subject of your message.

If there is a topic that you have expertise in and you are interested in either writing or contributing to a book, see our author guide on www.packtpub.com/authors.

Customer support

Now that you are the proud owner of a Packt book, we have a number of things to help you to get the most from your purchase.

Downloading the example code

You can download the example code files for all Packt books you have purchased from your account at http://www.packtpub.com. If you purchased this book elsewhere, you can visit http://www.packtpub.com/support and register to have the files e-mailed directly to you.

Errata

Although we have taken every care to ensure the accuracy of our content, mistakes do happen. If you find a mistake in one of our books — maybe a mistake in the text or the code — we would be grateful if you would report this to us. By doing so, you can save other readers from frustration and help us improve subsequent versions of this book. If you find any errata, please report them by visiting http://www.packtpub.com/submit-errata, selecting your book, clicking on the **errata submission form** link, and entering the details of your errata. Once your errata are verified, your submission will be accepted and the errata will be uploaded on our website, or added to any list of existing errata, under the Errata section of that title. Any existing errata can be viewed by selecting your title from http://www.packtpub.com/support.

Piracy

Piracy of copyright material on the Internet is an ongoing problem across all media. At Packt, we take the protection of our copyright and licenses very seriously. If you come across any illegal copies of our works, in any form, on the Internet, please provide us with the location address or website name immediately so that we can pursue a remedy.

Please contact us at copyright@packtpub.com with a link to the suspected pirated material.

We appreciate your help in protecting our authors, and our ability to bring you valuable content.

Questions

You can contact us at questions@packtpub.com if you are having a problem with any aspect of the book, and we will do our best to address it.

SQL Server 2014 and Cloud

1

Cloud is a buzzword that has been around for a long time, and it can in fact have many different meanings. Generally, it is considered as a process where remote computers are used to provide services possibly over the Internet, rather than using local computer servers or personal computers. A cloud can be public when computing resources are provided and hosted by a third party over the Internet and shared by all the paying subscribers, or private when computers and servers are hosted and owned by a company or business. A cloud can be **Software as a Service (SaaS)**, **Infrastructure as a Service (IaaS)**, or even **Hardware as a Service (HaaS)**. Microsoft's strategy seems to be pushing towards a cloud infrastructure, and SQL Server 2014 has some features that make hosting your data and/or infrastructure in the cloud easy to work with, set up, and manage. In this chapter, you will explore the options that are available when working with SQL Server in the cloud — Microsoft Cloud in particular. We will also look at setting up and configuring Microsoft Azure Storage to house your SQL Server data files and creating your own Microsoft Azure SQL Server virtual machines. You can find out more information about this at `http://azure.microsoft.com/en-us/services/sql-database/`.

In this chapter, you will learn about creating databases in Microsoft's cloud solution. This is called Microsoft Azure SQL Database, previously known as SQL Azure.

Windows Azure SQL Database

Microsoft has both an SaaS and an IaaS offerings, and we will look at each of these offerings in the following paragraphs.

SaaS is a centrally managed and hosted piece of software that you pay for like a utility bill. Usually, the data used or consumed is used to calculate how much you pay. The more you use, the more you pay. Windows Azure SQL Database (formerly known as SQL Azure) is an example of SaaS.

IaaS is a service offered by a cloud provider whereby the hardware is hosted by the provider and you pay for what you use, much like the utility bill analogy used previously. The physical infrastructure is managed by the cloud solution provider, but you do have some control over how the virtual machine running your software is set up. You don't need to worry about managing and maintaining the physical hardware, and IaaS can make it a simple process to scale out your environment. Microsoft Azure also allows you to host your own virtual machine, with the Windows Server operating system and SQL Server 2014 installed. Amazon offered IaaS, providing virtual machines with SQL Server installed for a long time. Microsoft has recently followed suit with Microsoft Azure Virtual Machines. You can host Active Directory services in the cloud too. This means your off-premise Microsoft Azure Virtual Machines can be integrated nicely with your one-premise physical or virtual machines.

Creating a Windows Azure SQL database

To create a Microsoft Azure database, we need a Microsoft Azure account, which you can get as a free trial if you want to experiment with Microsoft Azure. However, you will need to enter some credit card information, even if you only want the free trial. To create your account, visit `http://azure.microsoft.com/en-us/` and follow these steps:

1. When you have created your Microsoft Azure account, you will need to log in to the management portal. You will come across a screen that looks similar to the following screenshot:

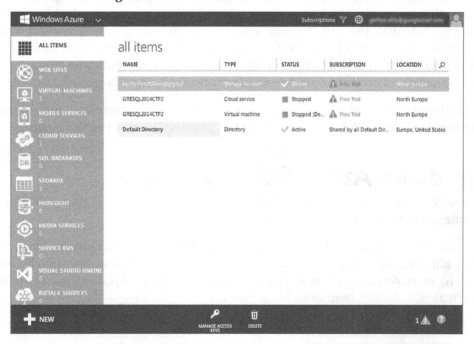

2. Click on the **SQL DATABASES** option from the menu on the left-hand side. If you don't have any SQL databases created, you will have a screen that looks similar to the following screenshot:

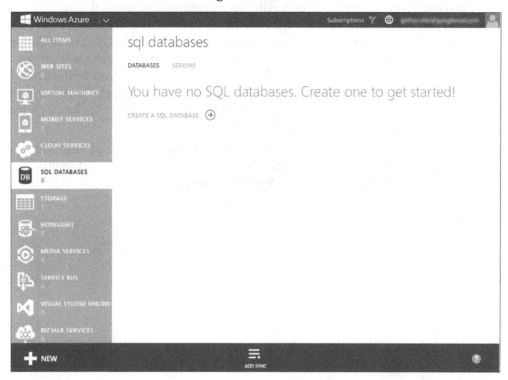

3. Click on the **New** button to start the **Create Database** wizard. You need to make some choices from the screen shown in the following screenshot:

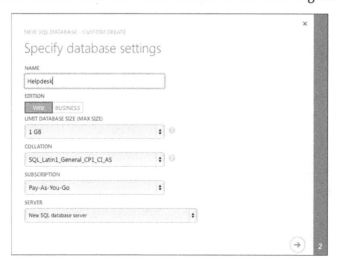

4. In this wizard, the database helpdesk has been called upon. The edition of the Windows Azure SQL Database defines what features are available and how much it costs. For the purposes of this example, a web edition database has been chosen. With the web edition of Windows Azure SQL database, you can have a database storage limit of up to 5 GB. If you chose the business edition, you can have a database storage limit of up to 150 GB. The next step is to choose the collation for your database, which in this case has been set to the default setting, as well as the subscription type that you wish to use to pay for your SaaS database. As a SQL database for Microsoft Azure is yet to be chosen, you need to select the **New SQL database Server** option. You then need to click on the next arrow button.

5. On the next screen, you will need to enter some server settings and then create a login name; in this case, I entered `Gethyn` and a safe and secure password. I chose my region as **Western Europe**.

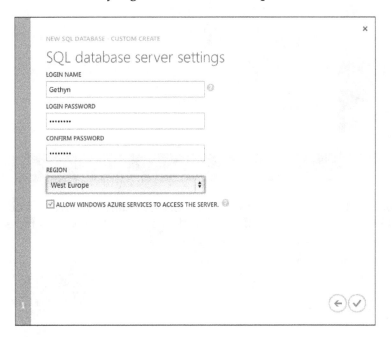

6. Click on the check box to create the Microsoft Azure database. Once the database has been created successfully, you can view it under the **SQL DATABASES** section in the Microsoft Azure management portal.

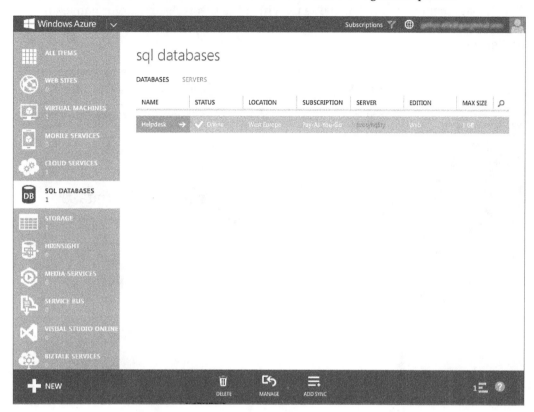

Connecting to a Windows Azure SQL database with Management Studio

Now that a Windows Azure SQL database has been created, the next step is to connect the database in order to begin the design process, which involves creating tables to store your important business data. SQL Server 2014 comes with Management Studio, which is a robust tool for both administrators and developers to code and administer SQL Servers and SQL Server databases. We can use this tool to work with our SQL Azure Database.

SQL Server 2014 Management Studio has been installed in this case; you can install Management Studio from the SQL Server installation media if it is not installed already. Installing SQL Server Management Studio is outside the scope of this book. The management portal will provide us with a Microsoft Azure server name, and you can connect it to the server using the username and password created in the earlier steps.

Before you connect, you will need to set up firewall rules to allow your laptop to connect. Click on the **Set up Windows Azure firewall rules for this IP address** link.

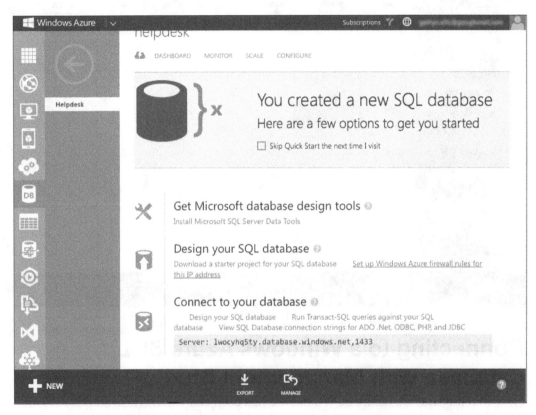

The firewall rule can take a few minutes to take effect. Fire up SQL Server Management Studio 2014 and connect it to the Windows Azure SQL Database. You will need to specify the server name given to you when you created your Windows SQL Azure Database and also the login name and password. Once you click on **Connect**, you will then be connected to your Windows SQL Azure Database. You will see that **Object Explorer** looks different in comparison to a local SQL Server instance connection. You have three folders available: **Databases**, **Security**, and **Management**. This is all you need.

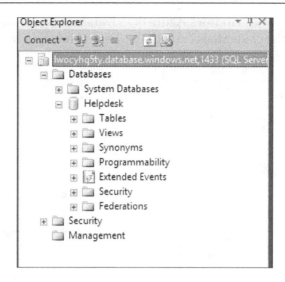

Migrating an existing database to Microsoft Azure

If you have an existing database on a local instance of SQL Server, there is a wizard you can use to help migrate a database to a Windows Azure SQL Database. In my case, I have a database called **T3** that currently sits on my local SQL Server 2014 instance. You can then use the management studio wizard to move the database to Microsoft Azure.

You need to connect to the local SQL Server 2014 instance in Management Studio. To start the wizard, right-click on the database to move. Select the **Tasks** option and click on **Deploy to Windows Azure SQL Database** to start the wizard. The first screen of the wizard explains what the wizard will implement; you can safely click on **Next** on this screen.

You will then specify the Windows Azure SQL Database server name; for this example, I will use the credentials I created earlier as shown in the following screenshot:

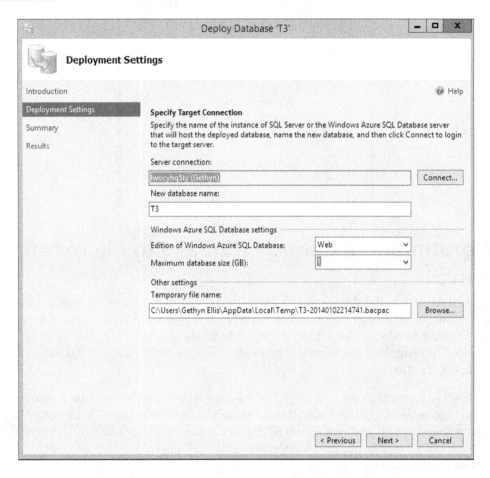

You will need the Microsoft data-tier application framework installed for your SQL Server 2014 wizard to successfully deploy your database to a Windows Azure SQL Database. A free tool to do this can be downloaded from the Microsoft website at `http://www.microsoft.com/en-gb/download/details.aspx?id=40735`.

When you have successfully deployed your on-premise database to a Windows Azure SQL Database, you will get a confirmation screen that reports whether the operation has been successful or not. You will be able to view the newly deployed SaaS database by connecting to the cloud-based SQL database in Management Studio.

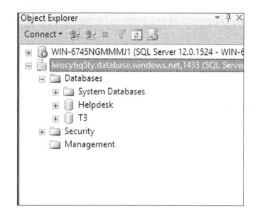

Integrating Microsoft Azure Storage

SQL Server 2014 offers you the ability to store your SQL Server data files in Microsoft Azure. This will allow you to combine on-premise and cloud-based storage solutions for your SQL Server 2014 databases. The files are stored as blobs in Microsoft Azure. This offers the DBA a number of benefits, some of which are listed as follows:

- Fast and easy migration
- Low cost storage — potentially limitless storage
- **High Availability (HA)** and **Disaster Recovery (DR)**
- Security

Creating a database that uses the Microsoft Azure Storage integration

In order to use Microsoft Azure Storage for your SQL Sever database files, you will need to create a Microsoft Azure Storage account, and you will need to create a storage container.

To create a database that uses Microsoft Azure Storage, you need to follow the ensuing steps:

1. Create a Microsoft Azure Storage account and then create a container.
2. Following this, create a policy on the storage container and generate a **Shared Access Signature (SAS)** key.
3. Now, create a SQL Server Credential.
4. Finally, you can create a database in Microsoft Azure Storage.

Creating a Microsoft Azure Storage account and container

To use Microsoft Azure Storage for your SQL Server database, an account and a blob storage container will need to be created. Because you have already created your Microsoft Azure Account, you will now need to create a storage container for the databases' data files.

From the management portal, select the **STORAGE** option from the left-hand menu, which is shown in the following screenshot:

Click on the **New** button at the bottom of the screen and run through the wizard. The most important thing to note here is that you need to disable geo-replication. When **geo-replication** is set, the write order is not guaranteed, and this can lead to database corruption. Geo-replication allows you to keep multiple durable copies of data across different sites, but how the technology writes data to disk does not lend itself to how SQL Server will write data to the disk. Therefore, when using Microsoft Azure Storage for your database, you will not be able to use this option.

Click on the **CREATE STORAGE ACCOUNT** button to create the account as shown in the following screenshot. The storage account will take a minute or two to do this.

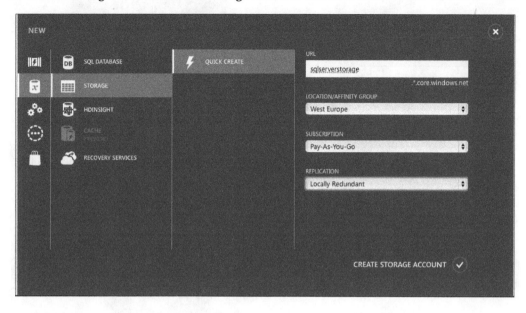

In the management portal, click on the newly created account that will be used for the storage configuration screen. At the top of the screen, you will see a list of options that contains **Dashboard, Monitor, Configure**, and **Containers**. Click on **Containers**, and click on the option to **create a container**. Give your container a name; I called mine `sqldata`.

The first step is complete; we then need to create a policy followed by SAS.

The container policy and Shared Access Signature

To simplify this process, Azure Storage Explorer is going to be used, which provides a nice graphical interface. You can download the software from the CodePlex website for free at `http://azurestorageexplorer.codeplex.com`.

After you have downloaded the Azure Storage Explorer, the following steps will guide you in using it to create a Shared Access Signature:

1. Install the `.msi` package on your computer, open up the **Azure Storage Explorer**, and connect to your storage container using the credentials supplied in the management portal. You will need the storage account that you created previously as well as a storage access key. Click on the storage account and then click on the **Manage Access Keys** icon. This can be found at the bottom of the storage container. You will need the key to connect.

2. When you have successfully connected to your storage account, the Azure Storage Explorer will look similar to the following screenshot:

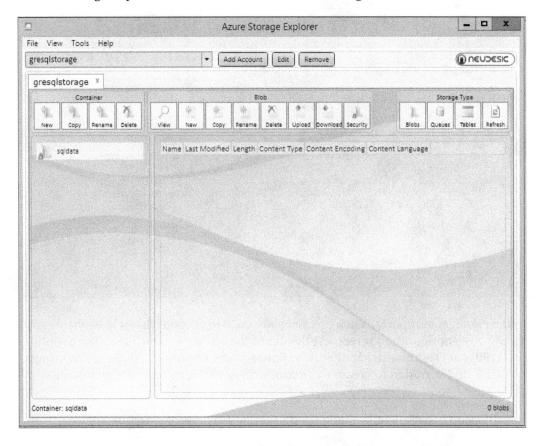

3. When successfully connected to the storage account, you will see the SQLDATA container on the left-hand side; click on the **security** button.

4. When the security dialog box opens, you will need to first create a new policy. Click on the **Shared Access Policy** tab.

5. Click on the **New** button and give the policy a name. To keep things simple, I called mine `sqldata` and gave policy permissions to read, write, list, and delete; along with this, you can also give it a start date, a start time, an end date, and an end time.

6. You then need to click on the **Save Policies** option. Following this, click on the **Shared Access Signature** tab, which is in the middle tab of the **Security** dialog box.

7. The **Container name** textbox should be completed. Leave the **blob name** text box blank and then choose the policy that was just created from the drop-down list. After this, click on the **Generate Signature** button. You will need this when setting up the credential in the next section.

Creating a credential

Connect to the local SQL Server instance in Management Studio that will be used to house the database that will make use of the Microsoft Azure Storage to execute the following CREATE CREDENTIAL statement:

```
CREATE CREDENTIAL
  [https://gresqlstorage.blob.core.windows.net/sqldata]
WITH IDENTITY='SHARED ACCESS SIGNATURE',
SECRET = 'sr=c&si=SQLDATA&sig=
  PtQi1NXUuJz%2BGCUkpdgEBS4o4Lo60FjTbfJ2dNx3XX8%3D'
```

Downloading the example code

You can download the example code files for all Packt books you have purchased from your account at http://www. packtpub.com. If you purchased this book elsewhere, you can visit http://www.packtpub.com/support and register to have the files e-mailed directly to you.

The CREATE CREDENTIAL statement uses the full **Uniform Resource Identifier (URI)** of the storage container for the credential name, including https:// address. The identity is mandatory and needs to be set as SHARED ACCESS SIGNATURE. The secret is the SAS that we created previously but not the full URI—everything up to the first ? needs to be removed.

Creating a database using Microsoft Azure Storage

To create a database that makes use of Microsoft Azure Storage, you will have to connect to the local database instance where the database will be created using Management Studio and Object Explorer. So, open a new query window and run the following CREATE DATABASES statement:

```
CREATE DATABASE TestDB1
ON
(NAME = TestDB1_data,
    FILENAME = 'https://gresqlstorage.blob.core.windows.net/sqldata/
TestDB1Data.mdf')
  LOG ON
```

```
(NAME = TestDB1_log,
    FILENAME = 'https://gresqlstorage.blob.core.windows.net/sqldata/
TestDB1Log.ldf')
GO
```

This command will create a database that appears to be an on-premise database housed on the SQL Server 2014 instance, but the storage of the data and log files is in fact on Microsoft Azure Storage. This is a true hybrid database that spans both on- and off-premise technologies.

Microsoft Azure Virtual Machines

In this next section, we look at Microsoft's cloud-based Infrastructure as a Service offering. It is possible to quickly create a fully blown Windows Server 2012 virtual machine with SQL Server 2014 installed. Instead of building a virtualized environment on your premises, you rent a virtual machine from Microsoft. This approach does mean that you will have to undertake more of the administration tasks when it comes to managing the guest operating system, but you don't need to buy additional hardware.

Creating a Microsoft Azure Virtual Machine

The following steps will create a Microsoft-Azure-hosted virtual machine:

1. First, you will need a Microsoft Azure account to be able to create a SQL Server virtual machine in it. You can usually sign up for a free trial, so it won't cost you anything to test this out. Assuming that you have the account set up and you are signed in, you will be able to create your own virtual machine.

2. From the Microsoft Azure Management portal, you need to click on the **Virtual Machine** tab on the left-hand side menu. Click on the **New** button. Ensure that the virtual machine option is selected and then click on the **From Gallery** button as shown in the following screenshot. Microsoft supplies a list of templates that you can make use of in order to quickly deploy a virtual machine of your choice.

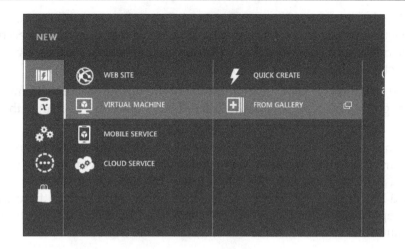

3. When you have clicked on **FROM GALLERY**, you can choose the template that you want to use. In this case, the **SQL Server** option has been chosen, so choose SQL Server 2014 on Windows Server 2012 R2. Then, click on the **Next** button as shown in the following screenshot:

4. Give the virtual machine a name. In my case, I have named my virtual machine GRESQL2014. Once you have chosen a name, specify an account username and password that will allow you to connect to the new virtual machine. Click on **Next** to continue.

5. You will then set up the configuration of the virtual machine. In my case, I'm going to accept the defaults offered here, but you can change them if you wish to. After this, click on **Next**.

6. In the next screen, you get to specify which endpoint should be created for your virtual machine; that is, you get to specify how you want to connect to and work with the new virtual machine. The defaults are Remote Desktop and PowerShell. Again, in my case, I am happy with both of these, so I will accept the defaults. However, you can add additional endpoints here if you want, too.

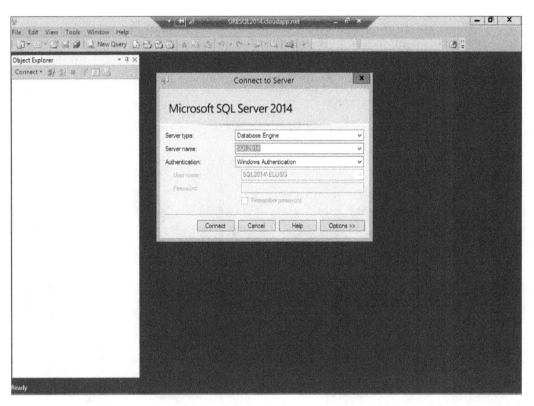

It will take a few minutes for Microsoft Azure to provision the virtual machines for you. When the machine is set up, you can set the remote desktop to the new virtual machine from your laptop or computer. From that point onwards, it's like working on any virtual or physical machine remotely. You can start Management Studio and connect it to your new SQL Server 2014 instance. You can create and manage databases just as you would with a server hosted in your data centers.

Summary

This chapter covered the new features of SQL Server 2014 that allow you, as the database administrator, to work with SQL Server on Microsoft's cloud platform. With the introduction of Microsoft Azure Storage for SQL Server database, the line between on-premise and off-premise has become blurred. Windows Azure SQL Databases offer a fully managed solution for housing your database. If you prefer, you can make use of SQL Server 2014 VM that is hosted in Microsoft Azure so that you, as the DBA, have more control and a greater ability to manage the server while the server is still hosted in the cloud.

In the next chapter, we will be looking at how the new features of SQL Server 2014 will help us develop a more comprehensive disaster and recovery strategy, and it's no surprise that there has been greater cloud integration in this area too.

2
Backup and Restore Improvements

We saw in the first chapter that the lines between on-premise and public cloud services have become blurred. The integration between on-premise and off-premise technologies imply that you can now easily implement a **backup** solution that makes use of both, thus allowing you to maintain up-to-date backups both on-site and off-site. This will allow you to implement a disaster recovery plan that meets strict service-level agreements without having to invest in a **Disaster Recovery (DR)** site. The DR site can be in the cloud. Depending on your environment, this can significantly reduce the cost of implementing a fully blown disaster recovery site or server room.

There are several new features in SQL Server 2014 that make this possible; they are as follows:

- Backup to URL
- Backup to Microsoft Azure
- Encryption

In this chapter, you will look at how you can make use of the new features and integrate them into your backup and recovery plans to ensure that you maintain up-to-date off-site backups.

Database backups to a URL and Microsoft Azure Storage

The ability to backup to a URL was introduced in **SQL Server 2012 Service Pack 1 cumulative update package 2**. Prior to this, if you wanted to backup to a URL in SQL Server 2012, you needed to use **Transact-SQL** or **PowerShell**. SQL Server 2014 has integrated this option into **Management Studio** too.

The reason for allowing backups to a URL is to allow you to integrate your SQL Server backups with cloud-based storage and store your backups in Microsoft Azure. You saw in the first chapter that you can now place your database files on Microsoft Azure cloud-based storage. By being able to create a backup there, you can keep database backups of your on-premise database in Microsoft Azure. This makes your backups safer and protected in the event that your main site is lost to a disaster as your backups are stored offsite. This can avoid the need for an actual disaster recovery site.

In order to create a backup to **Microsoft Azure Storage**, you need a storage account and a storage container. You have already learned how to create one of those back in the previous chapter when the SQL Server Database file was hosted on Microsoft Azure Storage.

From a SQL Server perspective, you will require a URL, which will specify a **Uniform Resource Identifier (URI)** to a unique backup file in Microsoft Cloud. It is the URL that provides the location for the backup and the backup filename. The URL will need to point to a blob, not just a container. If it does not exist, then it is created. However, if a backup file exists, then the backup will fail. This is unless the WITH FORMAT command is specified, which like in older versions of SQL Server allows the backup to overwrite the existing backup with the new one that you wish to create.

You will also need to create a SQL Server credential to allow the SQL Server to authenticate with Microsoft Azure Storage. This credential will store the name of the storage account and also the access key. The WITH CREDENTIAL statement must be used when issuing the backup or restore commands.

There are some limitations you need to consider when backing up your database to a URL and making use of Microsoft Azure Storage to store your database backups:

- Maximum backup size of 1 TB (Terabyte).
- Cannot be combined with backup devices.
- Cannot append to existing backups—in SQL Server, you can have more than one backup stored in a file. When taking a backup to a URL, the ratio should be of one backup to one file.
- You cannot backup to multiple blobs. In a normal SQL Server backup, you can stripe it across multiple files. You cannot do this with a backup to a URL on Microsoft Azure.

There are some limitations you need to consider when backing up to the Microsoft Azure Storage; you can find more information on this at http://msdn.microsoft.com/en-us/library/dn435916(v=sql.120).aspx#backuptaskssms.

For the purposes of this exercise, I have created a new container on my Microsoft Azure Storage account called **sqlbackup**.

With the storage account container, you will now take the backup to a URL. As part of this process, you will create a credential using your Microsoft Azure publishing profile. This is slightly different to the process we just discussed, but you can download this profile from Microsoft Azure. Once you have your publishing profile, you can follow the steps explained in the following section.

Backing up a SQL Server database to a URL

You can use Management Studio's backup task to initiate the backup. In order to do this, you need to start Management Studio and connect to your local SQL Server instance. You will notice that I have a database called T3, and it is this database that I will be backing up to the URL as follows:

1. Right-click on the database you want to back up and navigate to **Tasks | Backup**. This will start the backup task wizard for you.

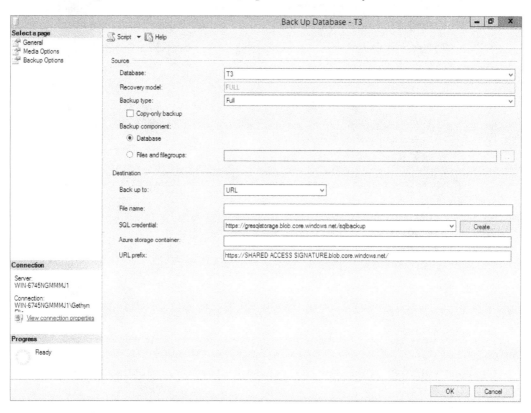

2. On the **General** page, you should change the backup destination from **Disk** to **URL**. Making this change will enable all the other options needed for taking a backup to a URL.

3. You will need to provide a filename for your backup, then create the SQL Server credential you want to use to authenticate on the Windows Azure Storage container.

4. Click on the **Create Credential** button to open the **Create credential** dialog box. There is an option to use your publishing profile, so click on the **Browse** button and select the publishing profile that you downloaded from the Microsoft Azure web portal. Once you have selected your publishing profile, it will prepopulate the credential name, management certificate, and subscription ID fields for you. Choose the appropriate **Storage Account** for your backups.

5. Following this, you should then click on **Create** to create the credential.

6. You will need to specify the Windows Azure Storage container to use for the backup. In this case, I entered `sqlbackup`. When you have finished, your **General** page should look like what is shown in the following screenshot:

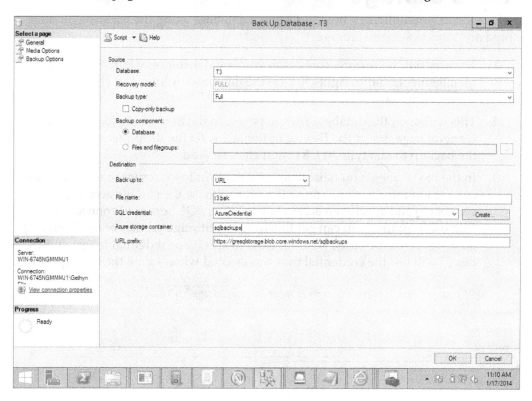

7. Following this, click on **OK** and the backup should run.

8. If you want to use Transact-SQL, instead of Management Studio, to take the backup, the code would look like this:

```
BACKUP DATABASE [T3] TO  URL
= N'https://gresqlstorage.blob.core.windows.net/sqlbackup/t3.
  bak'
WITH  CREDENTIAL = N'AzureCredential' , NOFORMAT, NOINIT,
NAME = N'T3-Full Database Backup', NOSKIP, NOREWIND,
  NOUNLOAD,  STATS = 10
GO
```

This is a normal backup database statement, as it has always been, but it specifies a URL and a credential to use to take the backup as well.

Restoring a backup stored on Windows Azure Storage

In this section, you will learn how to restore a database using the backup you have stored on Windows Azure Storage:

1. To carry out the restore, connect to your local instance of SQL Server in Management Studio, right-click on the databases folder, and choose the **Restore database** option.

2. This will open the database restore pages. In the **Source** section of the **General** page, select the **Device** option, click on the dropdown and change the backup media type to **URL**, and click on **Add**.

3. In the next screen, you have to specify the Windows Azure Storage account connection information. You will need to choose the storage account to connect to and specify an access key to allow SQL Server to connect to Microsoft Azure. You can get this from the **Storage** section of the Microsoft Azure portal. After this, you will need to specify a credential to use. In this case, I will use the credential that was created when I took the backup earlier.

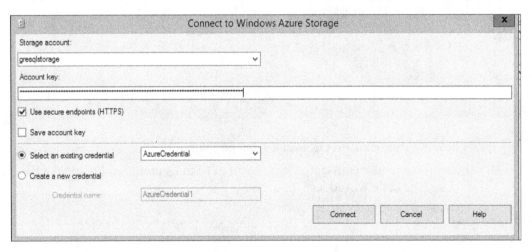

4. Click on **Connect** to connect to Microsoft Azure. You will then need to chose the backup to restore from. In this case, I'll use the backup of the **T3** database that was created in the preceding section.

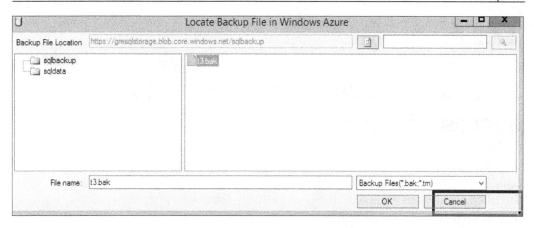

You can then complete the restore options as you would do with a local backup.

In this case, the database has been called `T3_cloud`, mainly for reference so that it can be easily identified. If you want to restore the existing database, you need to use the `WITH REPLACE` command in the restore statement. The restore statement would look like this:

```
RESTORE DATABASE t3 FROM URL = ' https://gresqlstorage.blob.core.
windows.net/sqlbackup/t3.bak '
WITH CREDENTIAL = ' N'AzureCredential' '
,REPLACE
     ,STATS = 5
```

When the restore has been completed, you will have a new copy of the database on the local SQL Server instance.

SQL Server Managed Backup to Microsoft Azure

Building on the ability to take a backup of a SQL Server database to a URL and Microsoft Azure Storage, you can now set up **Managed Backups** of your SQL Server databases to Microsoft Azure. It allows you to automate your database backups to the Microsoft Azure Storage. All database administrators appreciate automation, as it frees their time to focus on other projects. So, this feature will be useful to you. It's fully customizable, and you can build your backup strategy around the transaction workload of your database and set a retention policy.

Configuring SQL Server-managed backups to Microsoft Azure

In order to set up and configure **Managed Backups** in SQL Server 2014, a new stored procedure has been introduced to configure Managed Backups on a specific database. The stored procedure is called `smart_admin.sp_set_db_backup`. The syntax for the stored procedure is as follows:

```
EXEC smart_admin.sp_set_db_backup
    [@database_name = ] 'database name'
  , [@enable_backup = ] { 0 | 1}
  , [@storage_url = ] 'storage url'
  , [@retention_days = ] 'retention_period_in_days'
  , [@credential_name = ] 'sql_credential_name'
  , [@encryption_algorithm] 'name of the encryption algorithm'
  , [@encryptor_type] {'CERTIFICATE' | 'ASYMMETRIC_KEY'}
  , [@encryptor_name] 'name of the certificate or asymmetric key'
```

This stored procedure will be used to set up Managed Backups on the T3 database. The SQL Server Agent will need to be running for this to work. In my case, I executed the following code to enable Managed Backups on my T3 database:

```
Use msdb;
GO
EXEC smart_admin.sp_set_db_backup @database_name='T3'
, @enable_backup=1
```

```
,@storage_url = 'https://gresqlstorage.blob.core.windows.net/'
,@retention_days=5
,@credential_name='AzureCredential'
,@encryption_algorithm =NO_ENCRYPTION
```

To view the Managed Backup information, you can run the following query:

```
Use msdb
GO
SELECT * FROM smart_admin.fn_backup_db_config('T3')
```

The results should look like this:

	db_name	db_guid	is_availability_database	is_dropped	is_smart_backup
1	T3	EC8FBC88-A8D8-4613-BA41-1EAEBFB5B4A3	0	0	0

To disable the Managed Backup, you can use the `smart_admin.sp_set_db_backup` procedure to disable it:

```
Use msdb;
GO
EXEC smart_admin.sp_set_db_backup @database_name='T3'
,@enable_backup=0
```

Encryption

For the first time in SQL Server, you can encrypt your backups using the native SQL Server backup tool. In SQL Server 2014, the backup tool supports several encryption algorithms, including **AES 128, AES 192, AES 256**, and **Triple DES**. You will need a certificate or an asymmetric key when taking encrypted backups. Obviously, there are a number of benefits to encrypting your SQL Server database backups, including securing the data in the database. This can also be very useful if you are using transparent data encryption (TDE) to protect your database's data files. Encryption is also supported using SQL Server Managed Backup to Microsoft Azure.

Creating an encrypted backup

To create an encrypted SQL Server backup, there are a few prerequisites that you need to ensure are set up on the SQL Server.

Creating a database master key for the master database

Creating the database master key is important because it is used to protect the private key certificate and the asymmetric keys that are stored in the master database, which will be used to encrypt the SQL Server backup. The following Transact-SQL will create a database master key for the master database:

```
USE master;
GO
CREATE MASTER KEY ENCRYPTION BY PASSWORD = 'P@$$W0rd';
GO
```

In this example, a simple password has been used. In a production environment, it would be advisable to create a master key with a more secure password.

Creating a certificate or asymmetric key

The backup encryption process will need to make use of a certificate or asymmetric key to be able to take the backup. The following code creates a certificate that can be used to back up your databases using encryption:

```
Use Master
GO
CREATE CERTIFICATE T3DBBackupCertificate
    WITH SUBJECT = 'T3 Backup Encryption Certificate';
GO
```

Now you can take an encrypted backup of the database.

Creating an encrypted database backup

You can now take an encrypted backup of your databases. The following Transact-SQL statements back up the T3 database using the certificate you created in the preceding section:

```
BACKUP DATABASE t3
TO DISK = N'C:\Backup\t3_enc.bak'
WITH
  COMPRESSION,
  ENCRYPTION
   (
```

```
    ALGORITHM = AES_256,
    SERVER CERTIFICATE = T3DBBackupCertificate
    ),
    STATS = 10
GO
```

This is a local backup; it's located in the `C:\backup` folder, and the encryption algorithm used is AES_256.

Summary

This chapter has shown some of the new backup features of SQL Server 2014. The ability to backup to Microsoft Azure Storage means that you can implement a robust backup and restore strategy at a relatively lower cost. In the next chapter, you will look at what improvements have been made in the database performance arena.

In-Memory Optimized Tables

3

In many past versions of SQL Server, the general strategy from Microsoft has seen a great deal of improvement in the business intelligence stack. The database engine has remained relatively stable over these previous releases. SQL Server 2014 has seen a great new feature that has been introduced to help the DBA in the trenches. The production DBAs, who look after and manage transactional database systems supporting the day-to-day routine of trying to squeeze the last drop of efficiency out of their servers, now have a great new feature to help improve performance in the form of **In-Memory Optimized tables**.

During the pre-release of SQL Server 2014 this exciting new enhancement was called **Hekaton**. Hekaton is an old Greek word meaning one hundred or one hundred fold. Microsoft hopes that this new feature can improve performance and make certain transactions execute up to a hundred times faster than they do on the current platform. In this chapter, we will:

- Understand the system requirements of memory-optimized tables
- Consider how the new objects can work with virtualization
- Examine what you need to do to set up and create memory-optimized tables

Requirements

There are a number of requirements you need to satisfy in order to utilize In-Memory Optimized tables. These are as follows:

- In-Memory Optimized tables require the Enterprise edition SQL Server 2014 (the Developer and Evaluation editions also have all the features of the Enterprise edition but cannot be used in production environments)
- The SQL Server will need enough memory (RAM) to hold the data stored in the In-Memory Optimized tables

- If you are using disk-based tables, then you will also need enough RAM for the buffer pool

- You will need a processor that supports the CMPXCHG16B instruction set—all modern 64-bit processors support the CMPXCHG16B instruction set

Virtualized environments

It is very likely that you are working in an environment that is running at least some virtualized infrastructure and virtualized machines. It is also possible for the VMs to act as the server for your SQL Server 2014 instances. Due to the subtle difference virtualization offers over physical hardware, there are some additional considerations you will need to make. There are various best practices that have been suggested when running SQL Server on an enterprise hypervisor platform. The following excerpt is taken from the Microsoft SQL Server documentation also available at `http://msdn.microsoft.com/en-us/library/dn529286(v=sql.120).aspx`:

> *"Some best practices for virtualizing and managing SQL Server need to be modified when virtualizing a database with memory-optimized tables. Without memory-optimized tables, two of the best practices are:*
>
> *If memory pre-allocation is used with SQL Server, it is better to assign only the amount of memory that is required so sufficient memory remains for other processes (thereby avoiding paging).*
>
> *Do not set the memory pre-allocation value too high. Otherwise, other processes may not get sufficient memory at the time when they require it, and this can result in memory paging."*

If you follow this advice with memory-optimized tables, you can run into an issue when trying to restore the database or possibly even when your SQL Server gets rebooted or the service restarted. It is possible for the database to get held in a recovery-pending state. This is because SQL Server loads the data into RAM more quickly than the hypervisor's dynamic memory allocation provides memory to the database. To mitigate this risk when working with SQL Server memory-optimized tables in a virtual environment, set a memory reservation for the virtual machine on the hypervisor, thus ensuring that enough memory is allocated at startup. Consider that when setting a memory reservation, it can impact the VM being able to utilize some of the high-availability features that the Hypervisor can provide—such as live migration, which allows you to move a VM without taking the VM down or starting the VM on another node, should the current host fail for any reason.

Memory-optimized tables

The following quote is from the SQL Server 2014 documentation:

> *"SQL Server In-Memory OLTP helps improve performance of OLTP applications through efficient, memory-optimized data access, native compilation of business logic, and lock- and latch free algorithms. The In-Memory OLTP feature includes memory-optimized tables and table types, as well as native compilation of Transact-SQL stored procedures for efficient access to these tables."*

Much like traditional tables, memory-optimized tables offer fully durable transactions and meet **ACID** (**Atomic Consistent Independent and Durable**) by default and are designed to help databases that require really fast performance.

Much like the name suggests, memory-optimized tables are stored in the main memory (RAM) and therefore not on the hard disk. In fact, internally, SQL Server does keep a second copy on disk but this is for durability purposes and is only read from the hard disk during database recovery. A set of checkpoint files, data, and delta file pairs are used for recovery purposes.

The `insert`, `update`, and `delete` statements make use of the same transaction log that is used for the hard disk-based tables, so in the event of a server reboot, a crash, or the SQL Service being restarted, the transaction and the checkpoint can be used to repopulate the memory-optimized table.

In-Memory **OLTP** (**Online Transaction Processing**) supports delayed transaction durability, which means that soon after the transaction is committed, the transaction is written to the disk. This again offers a performance gain to the database administrator. There is no gain without pain though. To utilize this feature and to offset the performance gain, all the transactions that have not been written to the disk will be lost if the server crashes.

SQL Server 2014 also supports nondurable OLTP In-Memory Optimized tables. The data in the table is stored in memory but the data is not persisted to disk and data manipulation statements are not logged in the transaction log. Only the table schema is stored. This again can lead to dramatic performance gains but as always there is a trade-off and the downside is that the data will be lost in the event of a server restart. The database will also be lost in the event of an AlwaysOn Availability group failover.

We will need a memory-optimized filegroup to make use of memory-optimized tables. To demonstrate In-Memory Optimized tables, we will create a new database on our SQL Server 2014 instance that will use memory-optimized tables. When creating the database, you need to create a memory-optimized filegroup. The T-SQL command will create a database called InMemTab with a memory-optimized filegroup as given in the following code:

```
CREATE DATABASE InMemTabs
ON
PRIMARY(NAME = [InMemTabs_data],
FILENAME = 'c:\data\InMemTabs_mod1.mdf', size=500MB)
, FILEGROUP [InMemTabs_mod] CONTAINS MEMORY_OPTIMIZED_DATA( -- name of
the memory-optimized filegroup
NAME = [InMemTabs_dir],
FILENAME = 'c:\data\InMemTabs_dir')
, (NAME = [InMemTabs_dir2],
FILENAME = 'c:\data\InMemTabs_dir2')

LOG ON (name = [InMemTabs_log], Filename='C:\DATA\InMemTabs_log.ldf',
size=500MB)
GO
```

If you want to run this code, note that it uses the single file location c:\data. This has to exist if you want to run this script. Also, note that you have to separate out your data logs and location of the checkpoint files used in the memory-optimized tables in a production environment depending on how your storage is set up and configured.

When converting tables in the existing database, you have to create the memory-optimized filegroup using the ALTER database statement.

The Management Studio's database creation wizard has been modified to allow us to easily create a database with this new feature. When creating a database or working with database properties, you will see a new section on the filegroup page as shown in the following screenshot:

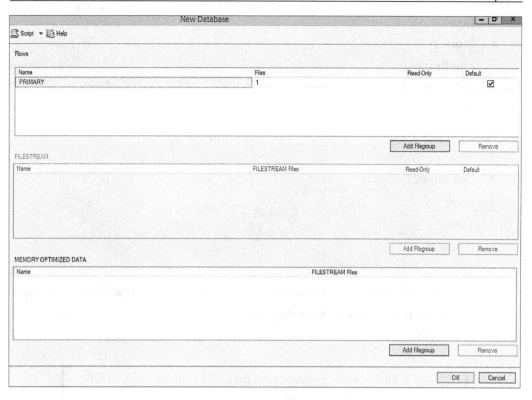

You have a database with the appropriate In-Memory filegroup; the next step is to create an In-Memory table. You will use a `create table` statement for this specifying the memory-optimized option in the `create table` statement. This is very similar to the syntax for creating disk-based tables. You will see we have used the memory-optimized switch so the database engine knows we want to create a memory-optimized table. By default, this will create a durable table, one that is also persisted to disk. The checkpoint files created as a part of durable are used in the event of a server crash and when combined with the databases' transaction log, can ensure that no data is lost.

There is a limitation on what data types can be used as column data types in memory-optimized tables. A memory-optimized table supports the following data types:

- Bit
- Tinyint
- Smallint
- Int

- Bigint
- Money
- Smallmoney
- Float
- Real
- Datetime
- Smalldatetime
- Datetime2
- Date
- Time
- Numeric
- Decimal Types
- All non-LOB string types: char(n), varchar(n), nchar(n), nvarchar(n), sysname
- Non-LOB binary types: binary(n), varbinary(n)
- Uniqueidentifier

 There can be no data types for XML, CLR, or MAX – LOB data types are not allowed.

There are several other limitations to consider when using memory-optimized tables given as follows:

- No FOREIGN KEY or CHECK constraints
- No UNIQUE indexes other than for the PRIMARY KEY
- No IDENTITY columns
- No DML triggers
- Maximum of eight indexes
- No schema changes when the table has been created
- No ALTER table, instead you would drop and recreate the table to make a change to its schema
- CREATE ALTER AND DROP indexes won't work either; the indexes get created as part of the `create table` statement
- Row lengths are limited to 8060 bytes, which get enforced during table creation

The following code will create a memory-optimized table called `t1 cart`:

```
CREATE TABLE t1 (
 T1ID int NOT NULL PRIMARY KEY NONCLUSTERED HASH WITH (BUCKET_
COUNT=2000000),
 UserId int NOT NULL INDEX ix_UserId NONCLUSTERED HASH WITH (BUCKET_
COUNT=1000000),
 CreatedDate datetime2 NOT NULL,
 TotalPrice money
 )
WITH (MEMORY_OPTIMIZED=ON)
GO
```

You can see here that when creating the table I have used `Memory_optimized=ON`, which tells the database engine when we want the table to be memory optimized.

You can insert rows to the table using native interpreted TSQL. You have two durability settings that you can use when creating a memory-optimized table: the `SCHEMA_AND_DATA` and `SCHEMA`. The `SCHEMA_AND_DATA` settings are the default settings so if you don't specify a setting, the memory-optimized table gets created as a durable table with data persisted to disk.

Memory-optimized tables and indexes

Memory-optimized tables support two types of indexes:

- **Non-clustered hash indexes**: These are used for point lookups.
- **Non-clustered indexes**: These are used for range and ordered scans.

Memory-optimized tables introduced a new concept called **hash indexes**. Hash indexes created on memory-optimized tables do not make use of a traditional b-tree structure like the one that the disk-based indexes utilize. Instead, the hash index is stored in a hash table with linked lists used to connect all the rows that hash to the same value, which are stored in Bw-Trees.

It is a requirement that a memory-optimized table should have an index created on it and this is demonstrated in the `CREATE TABLE` statement associated with the memory-optimized tables. An In-Memory Optimized table requires that `create table` must specify an index to be created. You cannot have an unorganized in-memory table like you can with disk-based heaps. You can see that we created a hash index from the sample code that created the `dbo.shoppingcart` table.

It is also worth noting that indexes on memory-optimized tables do not get stored on disk and are also not reflected in the checkpoint, data, and delta files. Also, index operations do not get logged to the transaction log. Indexes are automatically maintained when data modification statements are made on them much like their disk-based counterpart but in the event of a server restart, memory-optimized table indexes will get rebuilt.

Data storage for memory-optimized tables differs completely from its disk-based counterparts. Traditional pages are not used and the space is not allocated from extents. This is due to the design making use of the byte addressable memory.

Rows are allocated from a structure called a heap. This heap is different from the traditional disk-based heaps you associate with SQL Server tables with no clustered index created on them. Rows for a single table are not necessarily stored contiguously, that is, near other rows from the same table. The only way SQL Server understands which rows belong to the same table is through the index, since all rows are connected using the tables' indexes. Hence, the need and requirement of memory-optimized tables is an index. Each row will consist of a header and payload that contain the row attributes.

The row header will consist of two 8-byte fields that hold In-Memory OLTP timestamps called Begin-Ts and End-Ts. The value of Begin-Ts represents the timestamp of the transaction that inserted the row, and the End-Ts value represents the timestamp for the transaction that deleted the row. If a row has not been deleted, then its End-Ts value is set to a special value known as infinity. The header will also contain a 4-byte statement ID value. Every statement within a transaction has a unique StmtId value, and when a row is created, it stores the StmtId for the statement that created the row. If the same statement accesses the same row again, it can be skipped. The header contains a 2-byte value (idxLinkCount), which represents a reference count indicating how many indexes reference this row. The payload area is the row itself containing all the columns in the row including the key column, which in effect means that all indexes are covering indexes. A covering index is an index that contains all the data needed to satisfy the query.

Hash indexes are a type of index that can be used for memory-optimized tables. Hash indexes are basically an array of pointers. A hash index consists of a collection of buckets or containers organized in an array. A function is used to map the corresponding index keys to the containers in the hash index. The following diagram is meant to show how the hash function is used to determine which function contains the index key:

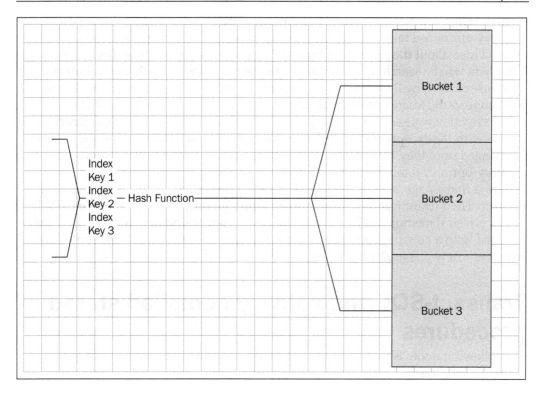

Each element in the array is known as a hash bucket. The key column of each row has a hash function applied to it, and the result of the function is used to decide which bucket a row is placed in. The hash function will be deterministic; the same index key will always map to the same hash index container and are linked together in a chain. When a row is inserted in the memory-optimized table, a hash function is applied to the index key value for the row.

When you create a hash index, you have to specify the number of buckets to create in the `create table` statement. Microsoft recommends that you choose a number greater than the number of the expected unique values of the index key column, so there is a greater chance that each bucket only has rows with a single value in its chain. It is also advised not to make the number of buckets too large as each bucket will use up memory. For details on the best practices to determine the number of buckets, please refer to the following MSDN article:

http://msdn.microsoft.com/en-us/library/dn494956(v=sql.120).aspx

Non-clustered indexes (non-hash) are another type of index that can be used with memory-optimized tables. You can possibly make use of the type of indexes if you have an idea about the number of buckets needed for a particular index or if you know you will be searching for data on a range of values. Non-clustered indexes make use of the new Bw-Tree data structure (for more information on Bw-Trees, you can read the Microsoft research paper at `http://research.microsoft.com/pubs/178758/bw-tree-icde2013-final.pdf`.) Bw-Trees have a similar structure to B-trees with the exception that the index pages are not of fixed size and they cannot be changed once they have been created. This is why you can't alter an index on memory-optimized tables. One big difference between Bw-Trees and SQL Server's B-trees is that a page pointer is a logical **Page ID (PID)**, instead of a physical page number. The PID indicates a position in a mapping table, which connects each PID with a physical memory address. Index pages are never updated; instead, they are replaced with a new page and the mapping table is updated so that the same PID indicates a new physical memory address.

Transact-SQL and natively compiled stored procedures

The following quote is from the SQL Server documentation on natively compiled stored procedures:

> *"Natively compiled stored procedures are Transact-SQL stored procedures compiled to native code that access memory-optimized tables"*

The process of having natively compiled stored procedures is a new feature of SQL server 2014 that is used in conjunction with memory-optimized tables. This allows for faster data access and more efficient query execution. There are some limitations to natively compiled stored procedures and the TSQL constructs they can make use of. The natively compiled stored procedures can only be used to access in-memory data.

The following code populates our `t1` table, which we created previously:

```
INSERT dbo.t1 VALUES (1,9000,GETUTCDATE(),NULL)
INSERT dbo.t1 VALUES (2,24,GETUTCDATE(),45.4)
INSERT dbo.t1 VALUES (3,81,GETUTCDATE(),NULL)
INSERT dbo.t1 VALUES (4,542,GETUTCDATE(),65.4)
GO
```

This will insert four rows into the `t1` table. You can use traditional T-SQL to retrieve data from the table too as shown in the following piece of code:

```
select * from t1
order by t1id
```

It is possible to convert these statements to natively compiled stored procedures. The following code creates a natively compiled stored procedure that selects data from the t1 table based on the users:

```
CREATE PROCEDURE dbo.usp_selt1 @userid int
 WITH NATIVE_COMPILATION, SCHEMABINDING, EXECUTE AS OWNER
 AS
 BEGIN ATOMIC
 WITH (TRANSACTION ISOLATION LEVEL = SNAPSHOT, LANGUAGE = N'us_
english')

 select t1id, userid, createddate, totalprice from dbo.t1
 where t1.t1id = @userid
 order by t1id

 END
 GO

 EXEC usp_selt1 1
 GO
```

The DLLs for the natively compiled stored procedures can be found in the following location for a default instance of SQL Server 2014:

`C:\Program Files\Microsoft SQL Server\MSSQL12.MSSQLSERVER\MSSQL\Binn\Xtp`

The following code will give you a list of all the In-Memory OLTP objects that have been natively compiled:

```
SELECT name, description FROM sys.dm_os_loaded_modules
where description = 'XTP Native DLL'
```

This code returns the name and location of the DLLs currently loaded into memory as can be seen in the following screenshot:

	name	description	
1	C:\Program Files\Microsoft SQL Server\MSSQL12.MSSQLSERVER\MSSQL\DATA\xtp\10\xtp_t_10_629577281.dll	XTP Native DLL	
2	C:\Program Files\Microsoft SQL Server\MSSQL12.MSSQLSERVER\MSSQL\DATA\xtp\10\xtp_t_10_597577167.dll	XTP Native DLL	
3	C:\Program Files\Microsoft SQL Server\MSSQL12.MSSQLSERVER\MSSQL\DATA\xtp\10\xtp_p_10_661577395.dll	XTP Native DLL	

The name of the DLL is prefixed with **xtp** and then a **t** or **p** depending on whether it is a stored procedure or table. In-Memory OLTP tables get compiled too and then derived from database_id and object_id.

Concurrency

Concurrency is the term used to describe how a database system such as SQL Server 2014 deals with multiple concurrent users. It is needed to ensure that when one person makes changes to the data, those changes do not adversely affect those of another user. This is sometime called concurrency control.

There are two types of concurrency control:

- **Pessimistic concurrency control**: A system-implemented locking system prevents users from changing data that affects other users. When a user performs an action, it causes a lock to be applied. The other users cannot perform any action that would conflict with that lock until that lock is released.

- **Optimistic concurrency control**: When reading data, users do not put locks on data. When a user makes changes to the data, the system checks if another user changed the data after it was read. If the data was changed, an error is raised.

- SQL Server supports a range of concurrency control. Users specify the type of concurrency control by selecting transaction isolation levels for connections or concurrency options for cursors.

Some concurrency terminologies

Some concurrency terminologies are listed as follows:

- **Dirty read**: Dirty reads can occur when a second transaction retrieves a row that is already being updated by a transaction. The second transaction reads data that has not been committed and may possibly be changed by the transaction updating the row.

- **Non-repeatable read**: Non-repeatable reads occur when a second transaction accesses the same row several times and reads different data each time.

- **Phantom read**: Phantom reads occur when a row insertion or row deletion action is performed against a row that belongs to a range of rows being read by a transaction.

SQL Server 2008 R2 and higher support the following transaction isolation levels:

- **Read uncommitted**: This allows dirty reads, non-repeatable reads, and phantom reads.

- **Read committed**: This doesn't allow dirty reads but does allow non-repeatable and phantom reads.

- **Repeatable read**: This doesn't allow dirty or non-repeatable reads but does allow phantom reads.

- **Snapshot**: This does not allow dirty, non-repeatable, or phantom reads.

- **Serializable**: This does not allow dirty, non-repeatable, or phantom reads.

All data access from memory-optimized tables will make use of optimistic concurrency. Multiple isolation levels are still allowed. In-memory optimized tables support the following isolation levels:

- **Snapshot**: In this isolation level, data reads will be a transactionally consistent version of the data that existed at the start of the transaction. Only committed transactions at the start of the transaction will be recognized. Data modifications made after the transaction has started will not be returned. With a snapshot transaction, the statements in a snapshot isolation transaction get a snapshot of the committed data as it existed at the start of the transaction.

- **Repeatable read**: This isolation level gives the same guarantee as the snapshot isolation level—you get a snapshot of the committed data at the start of the transaction. Along with that, you will get any row that is read by the transaction at the time the transaction commits, provided the row has not been changed by any other transaction.

- **Serializable**: Serializable builds on all the guarantees offered by repeatable reads and snapshot isolation levels and also prevents phantom reads. Phantom rows can appear between the time of the snapshot and end of the transaction. Phantom rows match the filter condition of a data manipulation statement. A transaction is serializable if we can guarantee that it would return exactly the same data at the end of the transaction as it did at the start.

Summary

In this chapter, we have looked at In-Memory OLTP. In particular, we have looked at in-memory tables, natively compiled stored procedures, how to create a database capable of supporting In-Memory OLTP, and how concurrency works with these new database objects. In the next chapter, we will look at Delayed Durability and how it can impact the performance of your databases.

4
Delayed Durability

In the previous chapter, we looked at memory-optimized tables, what you need to do to create them, and how they can help improve performance. In this chapter, we will have a look at another new feature in SQL Server 2014 that can also improve database performance, a feature called **Delayed Durability**. This makes use of an in-memory transaction log feature, which delays writing transaction log entries to disk.

Database theory suggests that relational database management systems and their transactions should be atomic, consistent, independent, and durable; often referred to as **ACID**. SQL Server makes transactions durable by writing transactions to its transaction log. If you suffer a bottleneck after writing a transaction to the log, your system can suffer from poor performance. SQL Server 2014 introduces the concept of Delayed Durability, which offers you (the database administrator) some control on how SQL Server writes transactions to the transaction log. However, be aware that if you change this setting, there is the possibility of losing some data in the event of a system crash or failure.

In this chapter, you will learn about:

- Full transaction durability
- Delayed transaction durability
- Full versus Delayed
- When should you use delayed transaction durability
- Delayed Durability and potential data loss
- Delayed Durability and other SQL Server features

Understanding the full transaction durability

Fully durable transactions mean that SQL Server will wait for a commit to be reported and the transaction to be written to the transaction log before returning control to the client. While it is waiting for the commit to be reported, SQL Server will block other transactions and sessions from accessing the resources it is updating.

Fully durable transactions will harden or write the transaction to the transaction log before returning control to the client. This is the default behavior in SQL Server. You should use this setting if you cannot tolerate data loss or poor performance in your system, which is not caused by write latency on the transaction log.

A fully durable transaction guarantees that once a commit succeeds, data changes made by the transaction are visible to other transactions in the system and durability is guaranteed on commit. The transaction is written to the log before control is returned to the client, which means that in the event of crash recovery running against the database, the transaction will not be lost.

Understanding the delayed transaction durability

Delayed transaction durability can reduce the waiting time caused by I/O throughput on the database transaction log. With Delayed Durability the transaction log records are stored in memory and written to the disk in batches, which in turn means shorter I/O wait times. The process is sometimes referred to as a lazy commit.

Delayed transaction durability uses a process of asynchronous log writes to disk. The transaction log records are stored in memory and are written to the log (hardened) when the buffer is full or a *buffer flushing* event happens. This process can reduce latency or wait time in the system along with reducing contention and the possibility of blocking in the system.

With Delayed Durability, the commit process does not wait for the transaction to be written to the transaction log (or hardened) before returning control to the client. Also, concurrent transactions are less likely to compete for log I/O. Instead, the transaction is stored in memory and written to the disk in larger chunks, which can result in reduced contention and increased system throughput.

The following is true for delayed transaction durability:

- When a transaction commit completes successfully, any changes made by the transaction are available and visible to other transactions in the system

- The durability of the transaction is only guaranteed when the in-memory transaction log is flushed to disk. A flush to disk can happen when:
    - A fully durable transaction in the same database commits successfully
    - The user executes the `sp_flush_log` system-stored procedure successfully
    - The in-memory transaction log buffer fills up, and then transactions are automatically flushed to disk

- It is only when the in-memory transaction is flushed to disk that the transaction become durable

Full Durability versus Delayed Durability

There are some factors to consider when deciding on whether to use Full or Delayed Durability. These include:

- **Data loss**: If you can accept some data loss and the performance of the system is more important than the recoverability of certain transactions, then Delayed Durability could be an option for you.

- **Bottleneck on transaction log writes:** After careful analysis of your system wait stats, you concluded that you are suffering from performance issues. This could be due to latency when writing to the transaction log, and you can accept some data loss in the event of a system crash or restart. In which case, Delayed Durability could be an option to solve this performance issue.

- **A high contention workload**: If your wait stat analysis shows that your performance slowness is caused by the delay in locks being released, then Delayed Durability could be an option. It helps remove the contention as it reduces the commit time and as such locks will be released faster.

For additional information on **Control Transaction Durability**, see:

http://msdn.microsoft.com/en-us/library/dn449490(v=sql.120).aspx

Using delayed transaction durability

You, as the database administrator, can control Delayed Durability at the database level and can set it using an ALTER database statement as follows:

```
USE [master]
GO
ALTER DATABASE [DB1] SET DELAYED_DURABILITY = ALLOWED WITH NO_WAIT
GO
```

This code changes the database option for Delayed Durability on the DB1 database from **Disabled** to **Allowed**.

You can also set this using Management Studio. Right-click on the database whose Delayed Durability settings need to be changed, and choose **Properties**, and then choose the **Options** page. You will see a list of options; scroll down until you come to the **Delayed Durability** option. There you will find a drop-down list with three options: **Disabled**, **Allowed**, and **Forced**. Choose the new value for the option and click on **OK** as seen in the following screenshot:

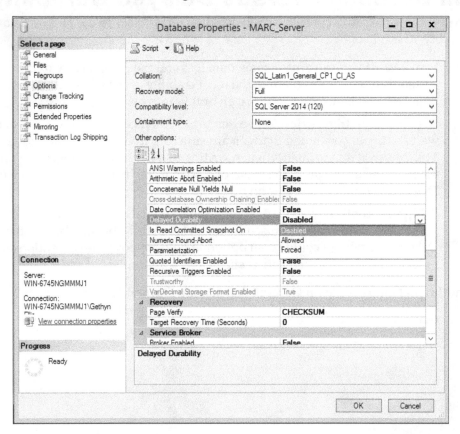

There are three options available to the DBA when setting the option for Delayed Durability:

- **Disabled**: This is the default setting. All transactions will be fully durable in SQL Server 2014 out of the box, unless you, as the DBA, choose the contrary. All transactions are fully durable regardless of any commit-level settings at the transaction level. This is the default setting and will prevent any unwanted data loss as a result of Delayed Durability. Yes, you read that correctly; it is possible to lose data using Delayed Durability. You would use Delayed Durability only when performance is more important than data loss.

- **Allowed**: If this option is selected, then the durability can be set at the transaction level. We will look at the `delayed_durability = on or off` statement in the next section.

- **Forced**: If you set the Delayed Durability setting to be forced at the database level, then all transactions, regardless of any transaction level Delayed Durability settings, will use Delayed Durability. This setting can be used when Delayed Durability will benefit the database as a whole. There will be no need to modify existing database or application code as long as you are happy to accept the potential data loss that could result in the event of a system restart or crash.

Transaction level Delayed Durability – Transact-SQL

If the database level Delayed Durability setting is set to **Allowed**, it means you can control Delayed Durability at the transaction level. The Transact-SQL syntax looks like this:

```
DELAYED_DURABILITY = { OFF | ON }
```

At the transaction level, the `DELAYED_DURABILITY` is either `ON` or `OFF`.

If the setting is set to off, which is the default setting, then the transaction will be fully durable. The only exception to this would be if at the database level the Delayed Durability has been set to **Forced**. In which case, the transaction will use Delayed Durability regardless of the transaction level setting.

If at the transaction level we set Delayed Durability to be on, the transaction will be delayed durable. The only exception to this would be if at the database level the Delayed Durability option has been set to disabled in which case all transactions would be fully durable regardless of the setting at the transaction level.

Delayed Durability and Natively Compiled Stored Procedures

When it comes to natively compiled stored procedures, the Delayed Durability switch will be much the same as the Transact-SQL equivalent. The official name for the Delayed Durability level is atomic block level control. The Transact-SQL syntax is the same:

```
DELAYED_DURABILITY = { OFF | ON }
```

The OFF switch means that the transaction will be fully durable unless the database Delayed Durability setting has been set to **Forced**. If it is set to **Forced**, the commit will be asynchronous and thus delayed durable and thus there is a risk of data loss.

The ON switch means that the transaction will use Delayed Durability unless the database option for Delayed Durability has been set to **Disabled**. If it is set to **Disable**, then the transaction will be set to fully durable regardless of the settings at the atomic block level in natively compiled stored procedures.

Much like the Transact-SQL equivalent, the setting used at the atomic block level will be determined by the setting at the database level. If you want specific transactions to be able to determine if they delayed durability, then you need to set the database option to **Allowed** for that granular control of the Delayed Durability setting.

The following is an example of the syntax needed at the atomic level to make a transaction using Delayed Durability:

```
CREATE PROCEDURE <procedureName> …
WITH NATIVE_COMPILATION, SCHEMABINDING, EXECUTE AS OWNER
AS BEGIN ATOMIC WITH
(
    DELAYED_DURABILITY = ON,
    TRANSACTION ISOLATION LEVEL = SNAPSHOT,
    LANGUAGE = N'English'
    …
)
END
```

Delayed Durability and transaction log flush

Delayed Durability means that it is possible that there will be transactions that have been reported as committed, and yet aren't written or hardened to the database transaction log. You know this and should be prepared to accept the potential data loss should the system crash or failover. But what if you need to take the system down for some reason? You wouldn't want to lose data as a result of planned outage. So, if your database is using Delayed Durability, you need some way of manually flushing the log to the disk. With SQL Server 2014, there are two ways to do this:

- You can execute the system-stored procedure called `sp_flush_log`. This will flush all committed transactions that are using the Delayed Durability option to the disk. To force a full flush of the in-memory log to the disk, execute the command `exec sp_flush_log`.

You can also execute a fully durable transaction that makes changes to the same database. This will also force a flush of committed delayed durable transactions to harden to the log.

To force a full flush of the in-memory log to the disk, you can execute the following:

```
exec sp_flush_log
```

Delayed Durability and potential data loss

In this section, you will discover how it is possible for you to lose data contained in a committed transaction using Delayed Durability.

The following script will create a database called DB1 on a SQL Server 2014 instance:

```
--Create database DB1
CREATE DATABASE [DB1]
GO
```

Then you will create a table in the DB1 database called t1. It will be a simple table with two columns called ID and Name:

```
USE DB1
GO
CREATE TABLE t1 (
  ID int,
  Name Varchar(20))
```

The following script inserts two rows into the table t1:

```
USE [DB1]
GO


INSERT INTO [dbo].[t1]
           ([ID]
           ,[Name])
     VALUES
           (1,'Seth'),
           (2,'Jake')
GO
```

The following script will change the database level Delayed Durability option to **Forced**. Therefore, all transactions will use Delayed Durability:

```
USE [master]
GO
ALTER DATABASE [DB1] SET DELAYED_DURABILITY = FORCED WITH NO_WAIT
GO
```

We will then set up a performance monitor and configure it to monitor log flushes. I am going to use the graphical tool for this but if you want to monitor for an extended period of time, you could set up a data collector. (Setting up a data collector is outside the scope of this book, but for more information you can visit http://technet.microsoft.com/en-us/library/cc749337.aspx).

To start performance monitor, search for performance and double-click on **Performance Monitor**.

Add the **Log Flushes/sec** counter to the live running performance monitor. This counter is part of the **SQL Server:Database** object of the monitor graphical user tool. The tool will look like the following screenshot. As you can see, this is not a busy database Delayed Durability has forced and there are currently no log flushes happening:

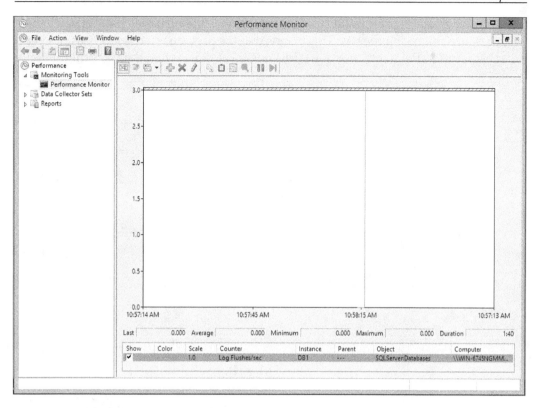

The following statement will update one of the rows in the t1 table. The code uses an explicit begin transaction and a corresponding commit. In previous versions of SQL Server, at this point you could be certain that the transaction had been hardened to the transaction log. The following code will insert a row into t1 using Delayed Durability:

```
begin transaction
update t1
set name = 'Seth Ellis'
WHERE ID =1
commit transaction with (delayed_durability = ON)
```

The following screenshot was taken after the update statement was run. As you can see, there are still no log flushes. This means that the previous transaction has not yet been hardened to the transaction log. Thus, there is a chance that data loss might occur:

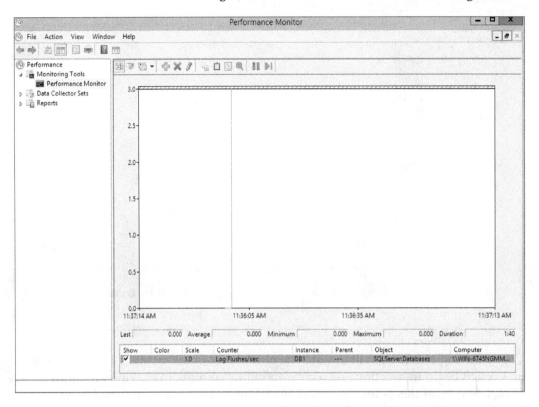

In order to ensure that the transaction and its data changes are hardened to the log and thus durable, we need to run sp_flush_Log:

```
Use DB1
Go
EXEC SP_FLUSH_LOG
```

This hardens the transaction to the log and you can view the log flush in
Performance Monitor:

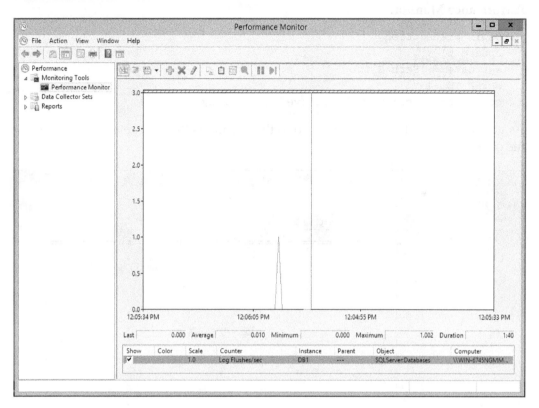

The spike in the counter indicates the log flush.

If the database's Delayed Durability setting had been set to **Disabled**, the log flush
would have occurred after the commit.

Next, the following script sets the Delayed Durability setting to **Disabled**:

```
USE [master]
GO
ALTER DATABASE [DB1] SET DELAYED_DURABILITY = DISABLED WITH NO_WAIT
GO
```

This ensures all transactions will be durable in the DB1 database. To prove this, we will run the following update statement and view the **Log Flush/sec** counter in **Performance Monitor**:

```
begin transaction
update t1
set name = 'Seth Ellis'
WHERE ID =1
commit transaction with (delayed_durability = ON)
```

As you can see, the transaction flushed to the log and is thus durable at the time of the commit:

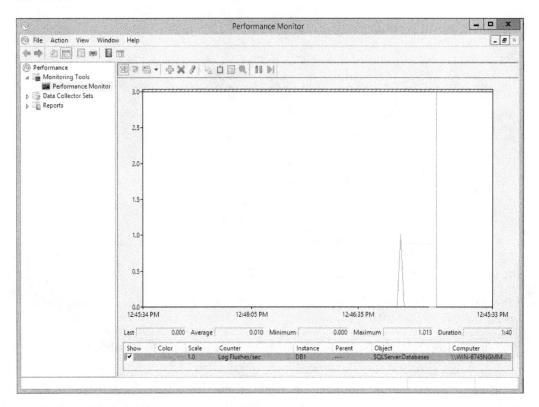

Delayed Durability and other SQL Server components

How does Delayed Durability integrate with the components of SQL Server? We will have a brief discussion here on how Delayed Durability will work with some other components of SQL Server.

Let's start with the most important: crash recovery. You, as the DBA, have no control over crash recovery. Crash recovery is the process that brings the database into a consistent state after the system has crashed for whatever reason. It is possible that changed data pages have not been written or hardened to the data file. In previous versions of SQL Server, they would have been written and hardened to the log-file as part of the commit process. With Delayed Durability in SQL Server 2014, its possible, using asynchronous commit, that transactions have not been hardened to the transaction log on disk and as such these transactions will be lost even though a commit was issued. The database will still be in a consistent state but potentially data will be lost. The following is a really useful TechNet article on understanding SQL Server logging and crash recovery: `http://technet.microsoft.com/en-us/magazine/2009.02.logging.aspx`.

AlwaysOn Availability Groups have been enhanced in SQL Server 2014 and you can combine AlwaysOn Availability Groups with Delayed Durability. Be aware that durability is not guaranteed on either the primary or secondary. In fact, it is possible that the secondary will not have knowledge of the transaction on primary until it hardens to the log. This is true for secondary setups in synchronous commit mode. In reality, if you are using synchronous commit mode with AlwaysOn Availability Groups, you are likely going to be using Delayed Durability on your database anyway — as data loss will be unacceptable. But it is worth pointing out that if you set up your database to use Delayed Durability, then you could potentially lose data in the event of a failover.

Much the same is true with SQL Server failover clustering. In the event of a failover, crash recovery will run on the second node when SQL Server starts up. If crash recovery runs and the transaction and its data changes have not been hardened to the log, then those transactions will be lost.

Transaction log backups will only contain transactions that have been made durable. So unless the transaction has been hardened to the transaction, they will not be included in the transaction log backup.

This leads us on to log shipping. If the transaction log backup only contains transactions that have been made durable, then it stands to reason that only backups that have been made durable will be shipped as part of log shipping.

Transactional replication will only guarantee the durable transactions will be replicated. So again, if you work in a heavily replicated transaction or peer-to-peer replicated environment, you will need to consider the data loss potential.

Summary

In this chapter, we have looked at Delayed Durability and how it can improve performance. It is important that when making use of this new feature in SQL Server 2014, you consider the potential data loss. Delayed Durability is something you should consider using if you have an I/O bottleneck or other related performance issues that Delayed Durability fixes. Always consider the potential for data loss and if that risk is acceptable to you. If the small amount of data loss that comes with Delayed Durability is not a problem for you, then this can be a great way of improving the performance of your databases. If, however, data loss, however small, is not acceptable to you, then this feature is not for you, regardless of the performance enhancement you can get from using it. In the next chapter, we will move on to the new high availability features and enhancements in AlwaysOn Availability Groups.

5

AlwaysOn Availability Groups

AlwaysOn Availability Groups was a new feature in SQL Server 2012 and was a major factor in certain shops while making the decision to migrate to SQL Server 2012. In SQL Server 2014, there have been some major enhancements and improvements in AlwaysOn Availability Groups. This includes allowing a replica to reside on Microsoft Azure Virtual Machine to help maintain replicas across different data centers, which have built-in disaster recovery as well, thus making use of the cloud, and also expanding the number of replicas that can be included in your Availability Group.

In this chapter, you will learn about:

- Availability Group enhancements in SQL Server 2014, including the fact you can have an eight node Availability Group
- Using Microsoft Azure Virtual Machines as replicas
- Troubleshooting Availability Groups
- Creating a hybrid Availability Group

Introducing AlwaysOn Availability Groups

AlwaysOn Availability Groups, introduced with the release of SQL Server 2012, are best described as enhanced database mirroring. It allows a set of user databases to failover automatically between different instances installed on separate servers; these are commonly known as replicas. Thus, it provides both high availability and disaster recovery, and applications that use these databases are automatically redirected; this minimizes the application downtime. From a disaster recovery perspective, multiple copies of the databases are maintained. So, if you have your AlwaysOn Availability Group replicas dispersed across different sites, then you can make use of the multiple database replicas for disaster recovery; if you lose one site, your database and its data are also stored safely on the other site or sites.

Enhancements in AlwaysOn Availability Groups

If you didn't know before, you must know now that you should have an understanding of what an AlwaysOn Availability Group is and what it can be used for. In this section, you will learn about what has been changed and enhanced in AlwaysOn Availability Groups in SQL Server 2014:

- **Microsoft Azure Replica** is one of the best features in SQL Server 2014. This feature gives the ability to have a replica hosted in Microsoft Azure. So, even if you don't have a second site that can act as a DR site, then you can make use of the cloud. Even if you have a DR site set up, you can have even more resilience by having a copy of your database at a third location—online—and satisfy your user requests.

- There has been a change in the number of replicas that you can have in your AlwaysOn Availability Group. In SQL Server 2012, you were limited to four replicas. With SQL Server 2014, this number has increased to eight replicas.

- If a secondary replica becomes disconnected from the primary, or if there is a quorum loss and the secondary setup must be readable, it will remain available for read-only connections during the disconnection.

- There have been some enhancements to troubleshooting issues with AlwaysOn Availability Groups in SQL Server 2104 including:
    - A new system defined function called `sys.fn_hadr_is_primary_replica`.
    - More helpful error messages and extended events.
    - More explanation of warnings in the setup wizard.
    - More information on data synchronization in the AlwaysOn Availability Group dashboard. You can examine some of these in the troubleshooting section.
    - There have been several enhancements in AlwaysOn Availability Groups in SQL Server 2014. We will look at some of them in detail in the rest of this chapter.

Using Microsoft Azure Virtual Machines as replicas

One of the new features of 2014 is the ability to combine your on-premise AlwaysOn Availability Group instances and also maintain a replica on Microsoft Azure Virtual Machine. This feature allows you to combine the flexibility and control of managing your own infrastructure along with maintaining a secondary stored site in the Microsoft Azure data centers.

The commit mode

Earlier in this chapter, we described AlwaysOn Availability Groups as database mirroring on steroids. Like database mirroring, AlwaysOn Availability Groups have two modes that you can choose from when configuring each replica:

The asynchronous commit mode: We can choose this commit mode when performance is more important than protecting against data loss. If every replica is running in the asynchronous commit mode, then the primary replica will not wait for any acknowledgement from the secondary replica that implies the transaction has been written to the log of secondary. This allows the database to run with minimum transaction latency, but it does run the risk of potential data loss. For example, if a transaction commits to the primary and there is a failover before the transaction writes to the log of the secondary, the data changes made as part of the transaction could be lost.

The synchronous commit mode: We can chose this commit mode if protecting the data is more important. With the synchronous commit mode, the primary replica will wait for all secondary replicas to acknowledge that the transaction has been written to their logs before completing the transaction. This ensures that all transactions and data are available on all the secondary replicas. This mode will have the highest transaction latency; therefore, it can have the biggest impact on database performance.

Reporting and administrating on secondary replicas

One of the big advantages that AlwaysOn Availability Groups have over database mirroring is that the secondary replica copies of the database are more useful to you. With database mirroring, the mirror copy of the database just sits there synchronizing. You cannot perform admin tasks such as backups on the mirrored copy. You can only run queries against the mirror if you make use of the database snapshot.

With AlwaysOn Availability Groups, you can configure your secondary replicas to be readable. This means that you can then offload your database's reporting requirement to the secondary database. With read-only routing, you can ensure that the client connections that specify a read intent connection get automatically directed to a readable secondary. You will need to have configured an Availability Group listener to achieve this automatic redirection.

AlwaysOn Availability Groups also allow you to run certain administrative tasks on the secondary databases. You can run the following tasks:

* Copy only full database backups
* Transaction log backups

You cannot currently make use of differential backups on secondary replicas. If you want to use differential backups on your AlwaysOn Availability Group databases, you will need to ensure that the differential backups are set up and configured to run on the primary database.

There is also a downside to creating a backup of a secondary. It adds additional complexity to your backup plan—you must ensure you know where your database backups are stored at all times, just in case you need them in an emergency.

Building AlwaysOn Availability Groups

To create an AlwaysOn Availability Group, you need the following:

* **Windows Server Failover Cluster (WSFC)**
* Enable AlwaysOn Availability Groups on each instance
* An IP address for the listener

Windows Server Failover Cluster

In order to make use of SQL Server Availability Groups, you need Windows Server Failover Cluster. The SQL Server instances will be standalone instances, and it is important to understand that AlwaysOn Availability Groups are not SQL Server clustering. In order to make use of the automatic failover and client redirection, the servers that will act as replicas in your configuration will need to be part of Windows Server Failover Cluster. This is not as traumatic as it sounds. There is no need for shared storage, we are not clustering the SQL Server instance, and clustering since Windows Server 2008 R2 is pretty painless to configure. If you are a DBA in a relatively large organization, there is a high possibility that you won't have the permissions to build up Windows Server Failover Cluster without the help of a Windows Administrator.

Thus, because of this, building Windows Failover Cluster is outside the scope of this book. For further information on building Windows Server Failover Cluster, visit `http://blogs.technet.com/b/keithmayer/archive/2013/02/04/step-by-step-building-a-windows-server-2012-failover-cluster-study-lab-in-the-cloud-with-windows-azure.aspx`.

Configuring the instance service

The nodes in an AlwaysOn Availability Group need to be able to communicate with each other. In order to do this, you can configure SQL Service to run as a domain account.

The SQL Server installation can take place before or after the WSFC can be built, but in order to configure the instance for Availability Groups, the nodes will need to be part of the WSCF.

AlwaysOn Availability Groups need to be enabled at the instance level, and this is done by configuring SQL Service using the Configuration Manager as follows:

1. Press the Windows key.
2. Find SQL Server Configuration Manager in the list of installed programs, and click on it to open Configuration Manager.
3. Locate SQL Service in the list, right-click on it, and select **Properties**.
4. Click on the **AlwaysOn High Availability** tab.

You will see the cluster name in the Windows Server cluster text box. Check the box to select **Enable AlwaysOn Availability Groups**, as shown in the following screenshot:

Click on **Apply** and then on **OK**. You will need to restart the service for this change to take effect. This process needs to be repeated on all instances that are involved in the Availability Group.

The Availability Group listener

The **Availability Group** listener is a key to allow your clients to be redirected automatically in the event of a failover. You can think of the listener as a DNS entry that points to the primary replica. In the event of a failover, the WSFC updates the DNS entry to point at the correct primary replica.

For the purposes of this exercise, I have created two virtual machines which will each act as a node in the AlwaysOn Availability Group. Each node will have 192.168.1.2 and 192.168.1.3 as their IP addresses, respectively. Each will be part of a WSFC called **AlwaysOnCluster** and will have 192.168.1.4 as its IP address, and the listener will be called **AlwaysOnDBL** and will have 192.168.1.5 as its IP address.

Creating Availability Group

With a Windows cluster built and each node configured for an AlwaysOn Availability Group, you will learn next to create an Availability Group in SQL Server 2014. You will then build the Availability Group and create a secondary replica using Microsoft Azure Virtual Machines.

On the instance you initially want to be the primary replica, connect in Management Studio's **Object Explorer**, expand the AlwaysOn High Availability folder, right-click on the Availability Groups folder, and choose **Always On Availability Group Wizard**. The first screen explains what the wizard will implement; click on **Next**. On the second screen, you will specify a name for your Availability Group; in this case, it is called AlwaysOnDBs. This can be seen in the following screenshot:

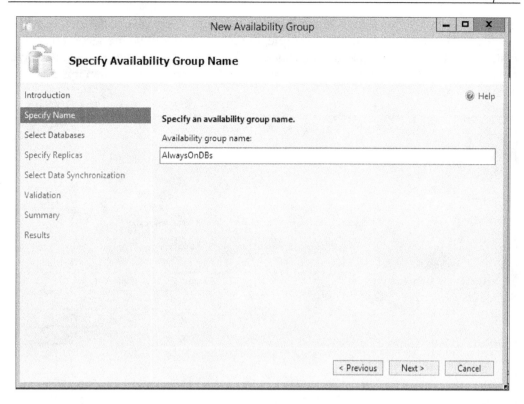

On the next screen, you will choose which databases to include in your Availability Group. In this example, two databases called DB1 and DB2 will form the databases in the Availability Group. There are some prerequisites for databases that can become part of an Availability Group. The pre-requisites include the database being in the full recovery mode.

On the **Specify Replicas** page, we will add in the first on-premise instance that will act as a secondary replica. In this example, the server that will be the secondary instance will be called **SQL2**. It is on this screen that you can configure the automatic failover and also check whether the instance is going be read-only when it is a secondary replica:

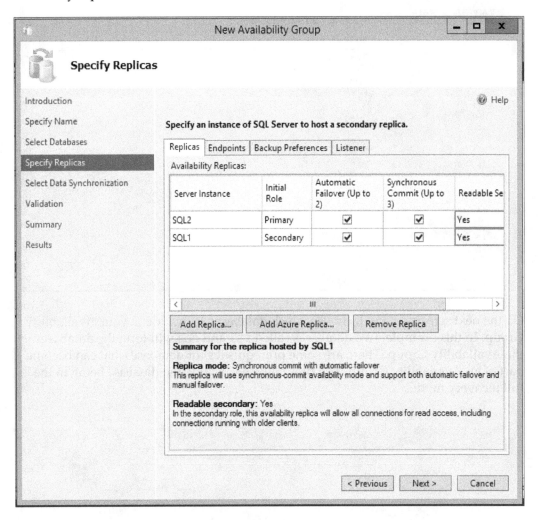

Note the other tabs available on the screen. The **Endpoints** tab provides you with information on what endpoints will be created when the Availability Group is created. Also note the **Backup Preferences** tab, where you can configure the preferences around the locations the Availability Group can back up. This feature has not changed since SQL Server 2012, so we will not look at it here. The last tab is the **Listener** tab that we use to create the listener for the Availability Group:

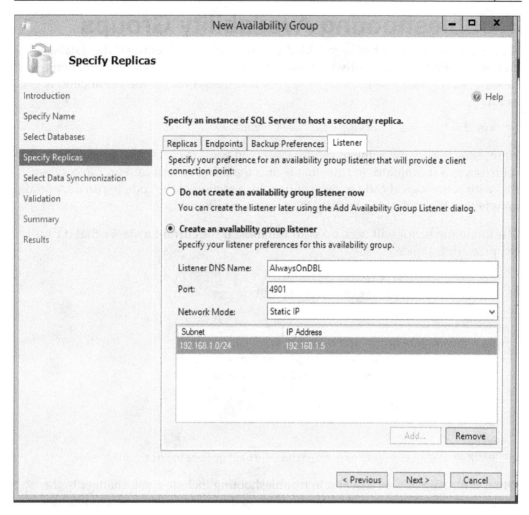

When you are happy with how the replicas are configured, you can click on **Next**.

On the next screen, you will have a choice on how the database will be initialized. For this example, you chose full synchronization. Click on **Next** on the **Synchronization** screen and some validation checks will run. They should complete successfully, and you can click on **Next**. Then, you can click on **Next** on the **Summary** screen and click on **Finish** for the configuration to run. When the wizard has finished, you will have created a new Availability Group.

Note that the databases on **SQL2** which is currently the primary replica are saying synchronized and under the AlwaysOn folder is our Availability Group AlwaysOnDBs.

Troubleshooting Availability Groups

A new system function has been added that will help you identify if the database and instance you are currently working on is the primary replica. The function is called sys.fn_hadr_is_primary_replica and the syntax for the is function is as follows:

```
sys.fn_hadr_is_primary_replica ( 'dbname' )
```

Here, 'dbname' is the name of the database you want to check. The procedure returns a 1, if it evaluates to true, that is, it is the primary replica. You can combine this with some logical code to determine which section of the code to run depending on whether the replica is currently the primary replica.

The following script will back up your database if the current instance that it runs is the primary instance:

```
declare @dbname varchar(30)
declare @backuplocation varchar(80)

set @dbname = 'DB1'
Set @backuplocation = 'c:\BACKUP\'
set @backuplocation = @backuplocation + @dbname
If sys.fn_hadr_is_primary_replica ( @dbname ) <> 1
begin
SELECT 'Nothing to backup'
end
else
BACKUP DATABASE @DBName to disk = @backuplocationIt
```

Other improvements in AlwaysOn troubleshooting include some changes to the dashboard. The AlwaysOn Availability Group dashboard allows you to monitor the state of your Availability Group.

You can start the dashboard by right-clicking on your Availability Group in **Object Explorer** and then clicking on **Show Dashboard**. You will see a screenshot similar to the following one:

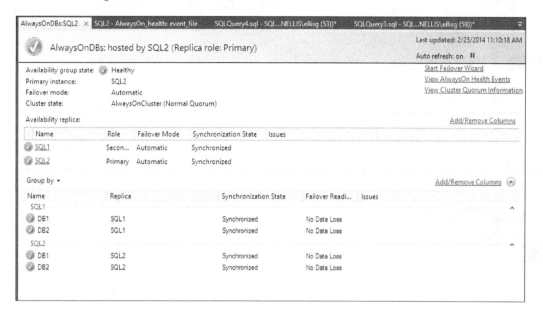

This is very similar to the dashboard in SQL Server 2012, but there have been some enhancements in SQL Server 2014. You can now add additional columns to give you extra information about the Availability Group.

If you click on the **Add/Remove Columns** link in the **Availability Replica** section, you can add columns that give extra information about your Availability Group. Click on the **Availability Mode** column to add it to the dashboard. This tells you which commit mode each replica is using. In the **Group by** section, click on the **Add/Remove Columns** link and add **Estimated Recovery Time** to the dashboard. This provides an estimate on how long the database will take to recover if it becomes primary.

Your dashboard will look similar to the following screenshot:

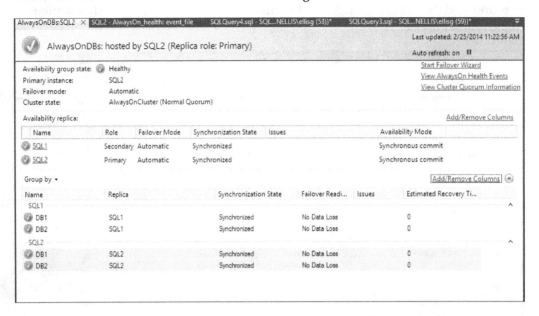

This additional information will be very useful to the DBA while making decisions about manual failover, how long it will take to recover, and how out of sync the secondary replicas have become.

Creating a cloud-based AlwaysOn Availability Group

We now have an on-premise Availability Group. With SQL Server 2014, it is possible to create an AlwaysOn Availability Group in Azure. You have two options: you can either create an availability that resides entirely in the cloud, or you can create a hybrid environment.

Creating an AlwaysOn Availability Group in Microsoft Azure

In this section, we will look at creating an Availability Group that resides entirely in Microsoft Azure. In order to configure this on Microsoft Azure, you need the following:

- A virtual network setup in Azure
- A storage account setup
- A Microsoft Azure domain controller
- WSFC
- One or more Microsoft Azure Virtual Machines with SQL Server 2014 installed and configured for AlwaysOn Availability Group

Build the Availability Group just as you have read in the previous tutorial. As you can see, in this case, it is the **Infrastructure as a Service (IaaS)** you have configured everything else. The following tutorial provided by Microsoft takes you through creating the necessary Microsoft Azure infrastructure.

Creating a Hybrid Availability Group

It is possible to combine on-premise and Microsoft Azure-based virtual machines to create a hybrid Availability Group. To do this, you need:

- A virtual network that contains multiple subnets, including a frontend and a backend subnet
- A domain controller and the SQL Server 2014 machines that you need to run behind a VPN device in your on-premise network
- A site-to-site VPN connection between the Microsoft Azure VPN device and your on-premise VPN device
- A SQL Server VM deployed to the backend subnet in Microsoft Azure and joined to your on-premise AD domain
- A WSFC multisite cluster with the **Node Majority** quorum model
- An Availability Group with two synchronous commit replicas on on-premise and one asynchronous-commit replica on Windows Azure

To add a Microsoft Azure Virtual Machine to the existing on-premise AlwaysOn Availability Group, when you have the infrastructure listed in place, you can right-click on the Availability Group and choose **Add Replica** to start the wizard. The **Add Replica** page will open and you need to select the **Add Azure Replica** option. Then, the following window will pop up:

You can now run through the rest of the wizard to add the Microsoft Azure Virtual Machine replica to your Availability Group.

Summary

In this section, you have learned about some of the enhancements and changes in AlwaysOn Availability Groups with the release of SQL Server 2104. These changes allow you to build up highly available solutions that consist of both on-premise and cloud-based replicas, which when combined can provided a high degree of flexibility and reliability while configuring your high availability solution.

In the next chapter, we will explore some additional performance features that have been added in SQL Server 2014.

6
Performance Improvements

In *Chapter 3*, *In-Memory Optimized Tables*, and *Chapter 4*, *Delayed Durability*, we looked at two of the new performance features in SQL Server 2014 that can help our systems perform more efficiently. There have been some other improvements and features added in this latest version of SQL Server that can also, if used correctly, help improve the performance of our databases. In this chapter, we will briefly look at some of these improvements and how we can make use of them to help us get the most out our databases.

We will be discussing the following topics:

- Partition switching and indexing
- Columnstore indexes
- Buffer pool extensions
- Cardinality estimator
- Statistics
- Resource Governor

Partition switching and indexing

With SQL Server 2014, it is possible for individual partitions of partitioned tables to be rebuilt.

In the following code example, we will rebuild a single partition, that is, partition number 5 of the IX_GETEST partitioned index on the dbo.t1 table:

```
ALTER INDEX IX_GETEST
ON dbo.t1
REBUILD Partition = 5
```

The ONLINE = ON option can also be used and now contains a further switch WAIT_AT_LOW_PRIORITY option that will allow you as a DBA to specify how long the rebuild process should wait for the necessary locks. The WAIT_AT_LOW_PRIORITY option will also allow the DBA to configure the termination of blocking processes related to the rebuild statement. This can be used in combination with the REBUILD Partition option.

Columnstore indexes

Columnstore index is a technology used for storing, retrieving, and indexing using the column data as opposed to the traditional row-based formats. Columnstore indexes were first introduced in SQL Server 2012 with certain limitations, and some of the limitations have been removed in SQL Server 2014. In SQL Server 2014, there is support for both clustered and non-clustered columnstore indexes, which is a change from SQL Server 2012 as it only supported non-clustered index columnstore indexes.

The SQL Server columnstore index differs from more traditional index types as it stores and manages data using the column-based data storage and column-based query processing. Columnstore indexes were initially designed to work well for data warehousing and decision support environments. In these types of environments, it's not uncommon that bulk loads run during an overnight batch processing job, when users are not accessing the system. During peak hours, the system supports read-only queries for reports. Columnstore index, if configured appropriately on the correct tables, can be used to achieve up to 10 times the query performance compared to traditional row-based storage and up to 7 times the data compression over the original data size.

Columnstore index offers a number of benefits, including the following:

- Columns often have similar data that is stored contiguously on disks. This can result in high compression rates.

- High compression rates improve the query performance as they have a smaller in-memory footprint; therefore, SQL Server can carry out more query processing in the memory.

- Columnstore indexes can reduce CPU usage. Batch-mode execution is a new query execution mechanism added to SQL Server that reduces CPU usage. Batch-mode execution is integrated with the columnstore storage format. This is sometimes referred to as vector-based or vectorized execution.

- A typical query will often select only a few columns from a table, which can reduce the total I/O from the physical storage, thus improving the overall performance again.

A quote from Microsoft on the columnstore versions at `http://msdn.microsoft.com/en-us/library/gg492088(v=sql.120).aspx` is as follows:

> *SQL Server 2012, SQL Server 2012 Parallel Data Warehouse, and SQL Server 2014 all use columnstore indexes to accelerate common data warehouse queries. SQL Server 2012 introduced two new features: a nonclustered columnstore index and a vector-based query execution capability that processes data in units called "batches." SQL Server 2014 has the features of SQL Server 2012 plus updateable clustered columnstore indexes.*

As mentioned in this quote, the clustered columnstore index can now be updated in SQL Server 2014.

Creating a clustered columnstore index

We can create a clustered columnstore index for a table using either TSQL or the management studio GUI.

Using Management Studio, connect to the instance of SQL Server that houses your database, expand the databases and tables, and right-click on the index folder to choose **New Clustered Columnstore Index**. It is worth noting here that if you have a normal rowstore-clustered index, you won't be able to create a clustered columnstore index. You can still only have one clustered index per table as shown in the following screenshot:

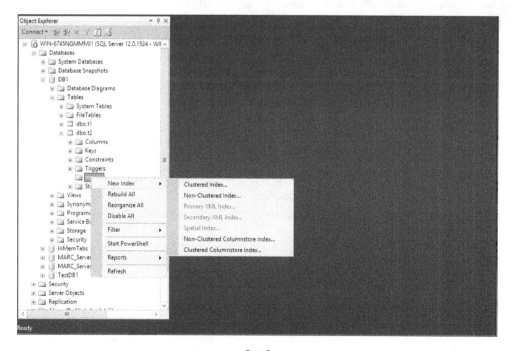

When the wizard starts, we will notice that there is no key column. it's also worth noting that all columns are included columns. It is also worth noting that the clustered columnstore index does not work with other indexes. If another index exits, you won't be able to create a clustered columnstore index, and if you have a clustered columnstore index, you won't be able to create another index type. Much like a normal clustered index which sorts and stores the data rows of table, a clustered columnstore index will store the data for the entire table. Clustered columnstore indexes are an enterprise-only feature in SQL Server 2014.

The transact-SQL statement for creating a clustered columnstore index is as follows:

```
CREATE CLUSTERED COLUMNSTORE INDEX
[ClusteredColumnStoreIndex-20140301-113651]
ON [dbo].[t2] WITH (DROP_EXISTING = OFF) ON [PRIMARY]
GO
```

You can issue a CREATE CLUSTERED INDEX statement that specifies the name of the columnstore index and then specify a name, the table to create it on, and specify a filegroup to create it on.

Updating a table with a clustered columnstore index

In the following example, a table named t2 has been created with two columns, aptly named C1 and C2. The code for creating the table is as follows:

```
CREATE TABLE [dbo].[t2](
   [c1] [int] NOT NULL,
   [c2] [varchar](50) NULL
) ON [PRIMARY]

GO
```

The code needed to create a columnstore index for the previous table is as follows:

```
CREATE CLUSTERED COLUMNSTORE INDEX
[ClusteredColumnStoreIndex-20140301-113651]
ON [dbo].[t2] WITH (DROP_EXISTING = OFF) ON [PRIMARY]
GO
```

You can see that the column C1 is using the int data type and the column C2 is using varchar(50).

If I run a simple select from the table t2, we will see that the table is empty, as shown in the following screenshot:

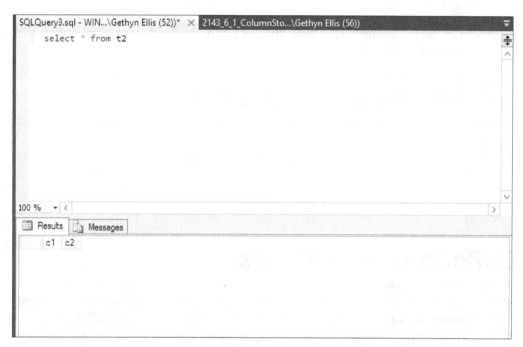

So, with the clustered columnstore index created, you would want to populate the table with some data. The following INSERT statement will insert two rows in the table:

```
USE [DB1]
GO

INSERT INTO [dbo].[t2]
        ([c1],[c2])
    VALUES
        (1,'Gethyn'),
       (2,'Seth')
GO
```

As you can see, we have two rows affected and the table has been updated. Now, turn on the execution plan (use the actual execution plan, not the estimated execution plan option) and run the following SELECT statement. Turn on the include actual execution plan to see whether the columnstore index is used to satisfy the following query:

```
SELECT * FROM t2
```

As shown in the following screenshot, the execution plan will show a columnstore index scan to satisfy the query:

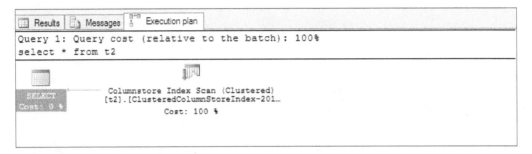

Buffer pool extensions

Buffer pool extensions allow you to make use of solid-state drives as extra RAM on your database server. They provide unified integration of a nonvolatile random access memory (solid-state drive) extension to the Database Engine buffer pool, which can significantly improve the I/O throughput. Buffer pool extensions are an Enterprise edition feature, so you have to pay the premium price for SQL Server Enterprise Edition to use this feature.

The main goal of a SQL Server database is to store, retrieve, and manipulate data. Therefore, you should expect higher disk access and disk I/O on many production systems. These disk storage operations can consume many server resources and take a relatively long time to complete; this delay can be the cause of performance issues that are caused solely by the I/O throughout. SQL Server, in order to counteract the delays that I/O operations can cause, has always tried to have an efficient I/O. It does this by making use of the memory or RAM. The buffer pool serves as the main memory allocation source for SQL Server. How the buffer pool is controlled and managed is a key component in achieving this memory efficiency and thus reducing the need for costly I/O operations. The buffer management component consists of two mechanisms: the buffer manager to access and update database pages, and the buffer pool to reduce the database file I/O.

Data pages get modified in memory, and the changed data pages are known as dirty pages. The checkpoint process, internal to SQL Server, writes the data pages back to the disk. Memory pressure on the server, along with database checkpoints, will cause dirty pages in the buffer cache to be removed from the cache and written to mechanical disks and then read back into the cache. SQL Server I/O operations are usually small random reads and writes of the order of 4 to 16 KB of data. Small random I/O patterns will incur frequent seeks, which will compete for the mechanical disk arm. This can reduce the I/O performance and reduce the aggregate I/O throughput of the system. It is the competition for the resources to carry out the mechanical disk I/O operations that can cause a system to become slow.

In the earlier versions of SQL Server, a reasonable approach to solving these I/O bottlenecks was to add more RAM, or alternatively, to add additional high-performance I/O spindles, or a combination of the two. These options are definitely helpful and are still likely to be helpful in SQL Server 2014. However, there are some drawbacks associated with them. These drawbacks are as follows:

- RAM is generally more expensive than data storage drives and adding extra spindles and disk drives increases capital expenditure in hardware acquisition. This can increase operational costs by increasing the power consumption and the probability of component failure.
- Mechanical disk drives can and will fail eventually.

The buffer pool extension feature allows SQL Server to extend the buffer pool cache by making use of **Solid State Drives (SSD)**. This enables the buffer pool to accommodate a larger database working set, which forces the paging of I/Os between RAM and the SSDs instead of the mechanical disk. This effectively offloads small random I/O operations from mechanical disks to SSDs. Because SSDs offer better performance through lower latency and better random I/O performance, the buffer pool extension can significantly improve the I/O throughput, thus removing I/O bottlenecks and speeding up the performance of a system. As I/O is usually the slowest component in SQL Server system operations, this will help increase the database performance.

The following code will enable the buffer pool extension on your SQL Server database:

```
ALTER SERVER CONFIGURATION
SET BUFFER POOL EXTENSION ON
    (FILENAME = 'F:\SSDCACHE\Example.BPE', SIZE = 50 GB)
```

Cardinality estimator and query plans

The cardinality estimator has been redesigned in SQL Server 2014. It has been redesigned in order to improve the quality of query plans and thus improve the query performance. The new cardinality estimator includes assumptions and algorithms that work well on modern transactional systems (OLTP) and data warehousing databases. Microsoft has made these changes based on customer feedback. The following is the feedback from a Microsoft customer:

> *while most queries will benefit from the change or remain unchanged, a small number might show regressions compared to the previous cardinality estimator.*

The changes to the cardinality estimator means that you should allow additional testing of your database as you migrate and move them to SQL Server 2014 to ensure that this change does not affect your database performance in a negative way.

Statistics

One of the problems while updating statistics on large tables in SQL Server is that the entire table has to be scanned, for example, while using the WITH FULLSCAN option to scan the entire table, even if only recent data has changed. This is also true when using partitioning. Even if only the newest partition has changed since the last time, the statistics are updated. Updating the statistics again requires a scan of the entire table, not just the current partition. This scan option includes all the partitions that didn't change. You can now update statistics incrementally with the introduction of SQL Server 2014, which can provide help with this problem.

The CREATE STATISTICS option and related statistic statements now allow for individual partition statistics to be created and updated using the INCREMENTAL option. Other related statements that allow or report incremental statistics include: UPDATE STATISTICS, sp_createstats, CREATE INDEX, ALTER INDEX, ALTER DATABASE SET, DATABASEPROPERTYEX, sys.databases, and sys.stats options.

Resource Governor

In the previous editions of SQL Server, the Resource Governor allowed you to specify the limits on the amount of CPU or memory that a process can use as part of the resource pool. In SQL Server 2014, this has now been improved with new Resource Governor settings to include the I/O activity too. In SQL Server 2014, you can use the new MIN_IOPS_PER_VOLUME and MAX_IOPS_PER_VOLUME settings to control the physical I/Os issued for user threads in a given resource pool.

Summary

In this chapter, we have discussed some of the new performance features of SQL Server 2014 that can help improve your database performance. We looked at partition switching and indexing, discussed some of the improvements in columnstore indexing, and looked at the enhancements in the Resource Governor and how changes to the cardinality estimator work. Hopefully, there is something that you can make use of from these improvements in your databases to improve their performance. As you can see, SQL Server 2014 has some great new features for the DBA. These new features will allow the DBA to implement a more robust and highly available production environment. The enhancements and changes to some of the SQL Server performance features, namely In-Memory Optimized tables and Delayed Durability, provide the DBA with an additional set of tools to get their databases performing at an optimal level.

Index

Thank you for buying
Getting Started with SQL Server 2014 Administration

About Packt Publishing

Packt, pronounced 'packed', published its first book "Mastering phpMyAdmin for Effective MySQL Management" in April 2004 and subsequently continued to specialize in publishing highly focused books on specific technologies and solutions.

Our books and publications share the experiences of your fellow IT professionals in adapting and customizing today's systems, applications, and frameworks. Our solution based books give you the knowledge and power to customize the software and technologies you're using to get the job done. Packt books are more specific and less general than the IT books you have seen in the past. Our unique business model allows us to bring you more focused information, giving you more of what you need to know, and less of what you don't.

Packt is a modern, yet unique publishing company, which focuses on producing quality, cutting-edge books for communities of developers, administrators, and newbies alike. For more information, please visit our website: www.packtpub.com.

About Packt Enterprise

In 2010, Packt launched two new brands, Packt Enterprise and Packt Open Source, in order to continue its focus on specialization. This book is part of the Packt Enterprise brand, home to books published on enterprise software – software created by major vendors, including (but not limited to) IBM, Microsoft and Oracle, often for use in other corporations. Its titles will offer information relevant to a range of users of this software, including administrators, developers, architects, and end users.

Writing for Packt

We welcome all inquiries from people who are interested in authoring. Book proposals should be sent to author@packtpub.com. If your book idea is still at an early stage and you would like to discuss it first before writing a formal book proposal, contact us; one of our commissioning editors will get in touch with you.

We're not just looking for published authors; if you have strong technical skills but no writing experience, our experienced editors can help you develop a writing career, or simply get some additional reward for your expertise.

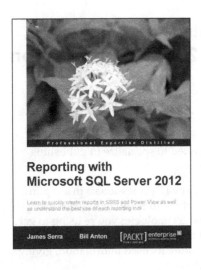

Reporting with Microsoft SQL Server 2012

ISBN: 978-1-78217-172-0   Paperback: 142 pages

Learn to quickly create reports in SSRS and Power View as well as understand the best use of each reporting tool

1. Empowers a highly visual design experience.

2. Increase productivity and proactive intelligence through operational or ad hoc reports.

3. Reporting with Microsoft SQL Server 2012 will cover all the features of SSRS and Power View and will provide a step-by-step lab activity to get you developing reports very quickly. You will learn the strengths and weaknesses of each tool so you understand the best tool to use for the various reporting scenarios you will encounter.

SQL Server 2012 Reporting Services Blueprints

ISBN: 978-1-84968-508-5   Paperback: 246 pages

Use real-world situations to develop real-world solutions

1. Detailed coverage of the various reporting options available.

2. Build end-to-end report solutions based on SSRS.

3. Learn from realistic situations to offer outstanding solutions.

Please check **www.PacktPub.com** for information on our titles

Learning SQL Server Reporting Services 2012

ISBN: 978-1-84968-992-2   Paperback: 566 pages

Get the most out of SQL Server Reporting Services 2012, both Native and SharePoint Integrated modes

1. Build applications using the latest Microsoft technologies: SSIS 2012, SSDT, WPF, and SharePoint 2010.

2. Reach out to the cloud and master Windows Azure Reporting Services.

3. Learn the ins and outs of SQL Server Reporting Services 2012 for Native and SharePoint Integrated modes.

4. Step-by-step learning, guided by a large number of screenshots in every chapter makes it a simple.

Microsoft SQL Server 2012 with Hadoop

ISBN: 978-1-78217-798-2   Paperback: 96 pages

Integrate data between Apache Hadoop and SQL Server 2012 and provide business intelligence on the heterogeneous data

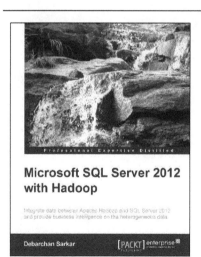

1. Integrate data from unstructured (Hadoop) and structured (SQL Server 2012) sources.

2. Configure and install connectors for a bi-directional transfer of data.

3. Full of illustrations, diagrams, and tips with clear, step-by-step instructions and practical examples.

Please check **www.PacktPub.com** for information on our titles